PRETTY-SHIELD
Medicine Woman
of the Crows

PRETTY-SHIELD

Medicine Woman
of the Crows

(originally published as *Red Mother*)

by FRANK B. LINDERMAN

Illustrated by Herbert Morton Stoops

UNIVERSITY OF NEBRASKA PRESS
LINCOLN AND LONDON

The John Day Company, 257 Park Avenue South, New York, N.Y. 10010. An INTEXT Publisher

Library of Congress Catalog Card Number 72-3273

International Standard Book Number 0-8032-5791-0

First Bison Book printing: March 1974

Most recent printing shown by first digit below:

8   9   10

Bison Book edition published by arrangement with Intext Press.

Manufactured in the United States of America

Dedicated to my grand-daughter,

SARAH JANE WALLER

I told Sign-talker the things that are in this book, and have signed the paper with my thumb.

FOREWORD

THROUGHOUT forty-six years in Montana I have had much to do with its several Indian tribes, and yet have never, until now, talked for ten consecutive minutes directly to an old Indian woman. I have found Indian women diffident, and so self-effacing that acquaintance with them is next to impossible. Even when Indian women have sometimes acted as my interpreters while gathering tribal legends they remained strangers to me. I had nearly given up the idea of ever writing the life of an old Indian woman when Pretty-shield delighted me by consenting to tell me her story.

Of all the old Indian women I know Pretty-shield would have been my choice, since in her the three essential qualifications for such story telling are in happy combination, age that permits her to have known the natural life of her people on the plains, keen mentality, and, above all, the willingness to talk to me without restraint. Besides these necessary qualifications Pretty-shield is a "Wise-one," a medicine-woman, of the Crow tribe. She not only belongs to a great Crow clan, the "Sore-lips" that has given her people many leaders and chiefs, but to a prominent Crow family. And there is yet another reason why I should have selected Pretty-shield, having written "American," the life of the aged Crow chief; Pretty-shield's story would be contemporaneous, since she is not more than eleven years younger than the Chief, and of the same tribe; and the tribe itself is ideal. The Crows (Absarokees), who are essentially plainsmen, have inhabited what is now Southeastern Montana for generations. They were constantly at war with the Sioux, Cheyennes, Arapahoes, and Blackfeet, so that nothing need be said of their ability as warriors. Their survival against such enemies, who greatly outnumbered them, is an eloquent proclamation that the Crows were brave.

Like the old men Pretty-shield would not talk at any length of the days when her people were readjusting themselves to the changed conditions brought on by the disappearance of the buffalo, so that her story is largely of her youth and early maturity. "There is nothing to tell, because we did nothing," she insisted when pressed for stories of her middle life. "There were no buffalo. We stayed in one place, and grew lazy."

Some of her stories are obviously tribal myths,

others "grandmother tales," and yet all, to the Indian mind, teach needed truths that may be obscure to others. Nothing is more bewildering to me than recording the dreams of old Indians. Trying to determine exactly where the dream begins and ends is precisely like looking into a case in a museum of natural history where a group of beautiful birds are mounted against a painted background blended so cunningly into reality that one cannot tell where the natural melts to meet the artificial.

Such a story as this, coming through an interpreter laboring to translate Crow thoughts into English words, must suffer some mutation, no matter how conscientious the interpreter may be (and Goes-together was conscientious). However, in this, as in all my work with Indians, my knowledge of the sign-language made it always possible for me to know *about* what Pretty-shield said, so that, even though she wished to do so, the interpreter could never get very far afield without my knowing of the divergence.

Anyhow Pretty-shield was all that I could have wished. If I have failed to let my readers know her the fault is mine.

F. B. L.

PRETTY-SHIELD
Medicine Woman
of the Crows

ONE

I WAS kindling a fire in an old-fashioned cannon stove occupying a corner of a room in the unused school building at Crow Agency when Pretty-shield entered with her interpreter, Goes-together, wife of Deer-nose, the Indian Police Judge. My back was toward the door, and besides this, the March winds from the plains rattled the window sashes so noisily that I did not hear the women's moccasined feet until they were by my side. I felt relieved. They had promised to come; but knowing the natural shyness of

Indian women I had been fearful that they might disappoint me.

"The day is cold," I said, casually.

"Yes," Goes-together answered. And then Pretty-shield spoke rapidly in Crow.

"She wants to know what it is that you wish her to tell you," said Goes-together, leaning against the wall.

"About herself, everything that happened to her since she was a little girl," I answered, putting chunks of soft coal into the wide door of the cannon stove.

"Ahhh! We shall be here until we die," laughed

Pretty-shield, her eyes merry. "Many things have happened to me. I am an old woman, Sign-talker."

"That is the reason why I want your story, Pretty-shield," I said, placing three hard-bottomed chairs beside a table. "I want only a woman's story, a woman who has lived a long time."

Seated, she watched me arrange my paper and a dozen sharpened pencils, her face again serious. I offered her a cigarette.

"No," she said. "My mother did not smoke, and I have never smoked."

Then, as though for emphasis, she drew her blanket more tightly about her ample shoulders. "And I do not know if whisky is sweet or sour," she added, a little bitterly, I thought.

"Talk signs to me, and Crow to Goes-together," I said in the sign-language.

Instantly her blanket fell from her shoulders. "Yes," she signed, her eyes telling me that she perfectly understood the reason for this request. She never forgot it. Her sign-language told her story as well as her spoken words.

Settling back in her chair, she let her eyes wander idly about the room, as though perplexed. I saw that a beginning was going to be difficult, that Pretty-shield felt out of place and might give up the task of story telling. I must lead her, by roundabout ways, to talk of herself, and must not wait. I would first question her a little about the social customs of the Crows.

"Tell me how a man treated a married sister-in-law," I suggested.

"Ahh, you know, or you would not have asked me," she laughed, so good-naturedly that I felt reassured. "A man was not permitted by tribal law to speak to a sister-in-law who was a married woman; and she could not lawfully speak to him. If either had a message for the other it must be sent by the woman's brother, if she had one, and if not, then by somebody else. Sometimes a man, and his woman, and a sister-in-law, and her man, had to live, for a time, in the same lodge, and yet this law was no different because they had to live together. It was the same with a man's mother-in-law. He could not speak to her, nor she to him; and they could not even sit together in the same lodge. This last law was not often broken; but the other one was sometimes forgotten."

"And a man who married a woman had the right to demand her unmarried sisters as his wives?" I asked.

"Yes, if he wanted them, and their relatives believed he could take good care of them," she said. "The women had little to say in this. A man, wanting a woman, would go first to her father, sometimes offering horses, sometimes nothing at all. The woman's father, if he thought the young man worthy, would talk things over with his relatives [clan] and then, if they agreed, the match was announced, a feast given, and a new lodge was set up for the young couple, even though the man might already have two or three lodges with women in them, and even children. If a woman's father had died, then her oldest brother acted in her father's place in all things pertaining to marriage. A man's parents always gave presents to his woman, when he took her, even horses, and fine clothing."

"Where were you born?" I asked, to get her started with her story.

"I was born across the Big [Missouri] river from the mouth of Plum creek in the moon when the ice goes out of rivers [March] of the snow that Yellowcalf, and his war-party, was wiped out by the Lacota [Sioux]." The rolls of the Old Agency show her age to be seventy-four.

"My mother's name was Kills-in-the-night. My father was Crazy-sister-in-law. There were eleven of us children. I was the fourth child to be born to my parents, who were respected people of the Crow tribe."

"And your name?" I asked.

"Little-boy-strikes-with-a-lance, my father's father, gave me my name, Pretty-shield, on the fourth day of my life, according to our custom. My grandfather's shield was handsome; and it was big medicine. It was half red and half blue. This war-shield always hung on his back-rest at night. In the daytime it nearly always hung on a tripod back of his lodge, which of course faced the east.

"No, a woman's name was never changed unless, when she was yet very young, she did not grow strong. If she was weak, and her parents were afraid that they might lose her they sometimes asked one of her grandfathers to change her name to help her."

"Do women ever name children?" I asked.

"Yes, sometimes," she said. "A wise-one, even though she be a woman, possesses this right. I named my own children, and all of my grandchildren. My Helpers, the ants, gave me all these names. I listen to the ant-people, even to this day, and often hear them calling each other by names that are fine. I never forget them."

She moved her chair, with a glance at the big stove that by now was heating the room. I closed the damper, wondering if this was the time to ask Pretty-shield to tell me her medicine-dream.

"My name was changed because I was sickly when I was a little girl," offered Goes-together, as I returned to my chair. "And I grew strong afterward," she added, soberly.

I could not imagine Goes-together as a puny child. She is stout, a fat woman, much heavier than Pretty-shield.

"Tell me of your girlhood, Pretty-shield," I said. "Begin with your first memories."

Now she smiled, her eyes full of fun. "We were a happy people when I came onto this world, Sign-talker. There was plenty to eat, and we could laugh. Now all this is changed. But I will try to begin with the first things I remember.

"About the time when I came to live on this world my aunt, Strikes-with-an-axe, lost two little girls. They had been killed by the Lacota; and so had her man. This aunt, who was my mother's sister, mourned for a long time, growing thinner, and weaker, until my mother gave me to her, to heal her heart. This aunt, Strikes-with-an-axe, was a River Crow. You know that because of a quarrel, just before my time [about 1832], the Crows divided into two tribes, the Mountain Crows, and the River Crows? Well, I was born a Mountain Crow, and this aunt was a River Crow.

"I can remember going away to live with my aunt, and the River Crows, although I could not have been three years old. This separation from my mother and my sisters was in fact not a very real one, because all the Crows came together often. These meetings gave me opportunities to see my family, so that I was happy, perhaps happier than I should have been at home. My aunt's lodge was large, and she lived alone, until I came to stay with her. She needed me, even though I was at first too young to help her.

"I well remember the first time that the Crow clans gathered after I had left my mother to live with my aunt. It was in the springtime. A crier, on a beautiful bay horse, rode through the big village telling the people to get ready to move to the mountains. His words set thoughts of again seeing my mother and sisters and brothers dancing in my young head. I felt very happy. Almost at once my aunt began to pack up; and then she took down her lodge.

"How I loved to move, especially when the clans were going to meet at some selected place, always a beautiful one." She turned to look out of the window at the wide plains, screened by the giant cottonwoods that surround Crow Agency, her eyes wistful.

"A crier would ride through the village telling the people to be ready to move in the morning. In every lodge the children's eyes would begin to shine. Men would sit up to listen, women would go to their doors to hear where the next village would be set up, and then there would be glad talking until it was time to go to sleep. Long before the sun came the fires would be going in every lodge, the horses, hundreds of them, would come thundering in, and then everybody was very busy. Down would come the lodges, packs would be made, travois loaded. Ho! Away we would go, following the men, to some new camping ground, with our children playing around us. It was good hard work to get things packed up, and moving; and it was hard, fast work to get them in shape again, after we camped. But in between these times we rested on our traveling horses. Yes, and we women visited while we traveled. There was plenty of room on the plains then, so that many could ride abreast if they wished to. There was always danger of attack by our enemies, so that far ahead, on both sides, and behind us, there were our wolves who guarded us against surprise as we traveled. The men were ever watching these wolves, and we women constantly watched the men.

"I have been dreaming," she said, smiling, "not telling stories. I will try to stay awake after this."

Just here a boy of about sixteen years entered the room with an air of assurance. Decked out in the latest style of the "movie" cowboy, ten-gallon hat, leather cuffs and all, he approached Pretty-shield, spoke a few words to her in Crow, and then stood waiting while the old woman dug down into a hidden pouch for a silver dollar, which she gave him without a word.

"My grandson," said Pretty-shield, when the boy had gone. "I have told you that I have raised two families of grandchildren. This one is of the first lot. They never get over *needing* me, though," she smiled, her kind face again merry.

"I wonder how my grandchildren will turn out," she said, half to herself, a dazed look coming into her eyes. "They have only me, an old woman, to guide them, and plenty of others to lead them into bad ways. The young do not listen to the old ones now, as they used to when I was young. I worry about this, sometimes. I may have to leave my grandchildren any day now."

"Did you ever whip your own children?" I asked.

"No, Sign-talker, you know that my people never did such things. We talked to our children, told them things they needed to know, but we never struck a child, never."

She stopped short, her lips pressed tightly together. "Lately I *did* strike a child," she said, grimly. "There seemed to be nothing else to do. Times and children have changed so. One of my grand-daughters ran off to a dance with a bad young man after I had told her that she must not go. I went after her. It was a long way, too, but I got her, and in time. I brought her home to my place, and used a saddle-strap on her. I struck hard, Sign-talker. I hope it helped her, and yet I felt ashamed of striking my grandchild. I am trying to live a life that I do not understand.

"Young people know nothing about our old customs, and even if they wished to learn there is nobody now to teach them. I believe that you know more about our old ways than any other man of your age, Crow or white man. This is the reason why I hide nothing from you. I have even spoken the names of the dead, which you know we Crows never do. Ask me anything you wish to know, and I will tell you, truthfully, Sign-talker."

"You were telling about the time the Crow clans gathered."

"Ahhh, we moved to the mountains," she murmured, her hands keeping up with her spoken words, "and when we reached the big village what a fine time we had! The meat! Fat meat, and dancing! I can hear the drums and the singing even now, and see the men dancing. My mother took me to her lodge, told me that I had grown tall, and gave me a doll and some pemmican. Tst, tst, tst, I undressed and dressed the doll until I wore it out. I played for days with my sisters on the green plains near the high mountains, and yet I do not remember that I felt sad when the clans separated again and I went away to the Big river with my aunt."

"What is your clan?" I asked, myself feeling the old love of moving camp.

"I am a Sore-lip [Burned-mouth, sun-burned lips]," she answered, her eyes lingering on the plains.

Plenty-coups, the aged Crow chief, is a Burned-mouth, a "Sore-lip." And now I noticed how much Pretty-shield resembled him. She has the same wide, fighting forehead, deep chest, and powerful body.

"Do you know where the Crows came from?" I asked, this being a question that I have put to many aged Crows.

"Yes," she answered, mistaking my question, "we came from *Magah-hawathus* [Man-alone, or Lone-man]. He made us, gave us our language, which is different from the others; and He made our enemies, as well. He told us that we should always have to fight to hold our country, but said that He would always be with us, because we would be out-numbered. And He kept His promise, or we should have long ago been wiped out."

"What does Absarokee [their tribal name] mean?" I asked, even though I knew her answer.

"E-sahca-wata [Old-man-coyote] gave us this name. We do not know what it means. He did not tell us. I never saw a man or woman who knew the meaning of Absarokee. Did you, Sign-talker?" she asked, eagerly.

"No," I told her, remembering the many attempts at its translation by competent Crows.

TWO

"WE Crows could not all live together," Pretty-shield went on. "The clans were scattered over the Crow country, so that all might find plenty of meat. The great herds of buffalo were constantly moving, and of course we moved when they did. I never tired of moving."

She leaned forward, her fine eyes softened. "I tried to be like my mother, and like another woman, besides, a woman that I shall tell you about. I carried my doll on my back just as mothers carry their babies; and besides this I had a little tepee [lodge] that I pitched whenever my aunt pitched hers. It was made exactly like my aunt's, had the same number of poles, only of course my tepee was very small. My horse dragged the poles and packed the lodge-skin, so that I often beat my aunt in setting up my lodge, which she pretended made her jealous. And how I used to hurry in setting up my lodge, so that I might have a fire going inside it before my aunt could kindle one in hers! I did not know it then, but now I feel sure that she often let me beat her just to encourage me. Each year, as was our custom, I made myself a new lodge and set it up, as the grownups did, when we went into our winter camps. Each time I made a new one I cut my lodge-skin larger than the old one, took more and more pains to have it pretty. I played with these little lodges, often lived in them, until I was a married woman, and even after. I have never lost my love for play.

"Once several of us girls made ourselves a play-village with our tiny tepees. Of course our children were dolls, and our horses dogs, and yet we managed to make our village look very real, so real that we thought we ought to have some meat to cook. We decided to kill it ourselves. A girl named Beaver-that-passes and I said we would be the hunters, that we would go out to a buffalo herd that was in sight and kill a calf. Knowing that we could not handle a bow, Beaver-that-passes borrowed her father's lance that was very sharp, and longer than both our bodies put together. We caught and saddled two gentle pack-horses; and both the old fools went crazy before we managed to kill a calf. I helped all I could, but it was Beaver-that-passes who wounded a big calf that gave us both a lot of trouble before we finally got it down, and dead. I hurt my leg, and Beaver-that-passes cut her hand with the lance. The calf itself looked pretty bad by the time we got it to our play-village. But we had a big feast, and forgot our hurts.

"And that night," she went on, her eyes happy, "we had great fun. The moon was big, as big as it ever gets, and very white. The lodges in the big village made pretty shadows, and everywhere people were laughing. The night was just chilly enough so that fires were burning in all the lodges. To make them smoke and bother the old people we girls stole about the village pulling the poles out of the smoke-ears of the lodges, letting them fall down. This was sure to bring some woman out to scold the moon-shadows, because she could not see *us*. One old woman pretended that she saw us, running straight at us with her root-digger in her hand. Tst, tst, tst! The things she said! But we stood still knowing that she could not see us unless we moved. I was glad when that old woman fixed her smoke-ears, and went back into her lodge. It is difficult to stand still that way when you are not exactly sure of yourself."

The two "flies" at the top of an Indian lodge govern the draught of the fire inside. The Indians call them "ears."

"And sometimes," she went on as though vivid re-membrances of her girlhood had suddenly come to her, "we made ourselves into mud-clowns and entertained the village, riding double on old horses that we made to look as funny as ourselves. There was one old man who would always drum for us, because drumming is not for women; and we would sing and dance through the village, stopping to show off before the lodges of our particular friends. Often women would come out and as though to pay us for our performances, give us meat and berries to eat."

The Crows are fond of clowning. With mud alone they are able to transform themselves, and even their horses, into grotesque figures.

"And once," said Pretty-shield, leaning toward me, her voice almost a whisper, "another girl and I robbed a dead Lacota," she confided. "Tst, tst, tst! We found him in a nice lodge that his people had pitched for his burial place. Pretending that we had killed this Lacota, we painted our faces black, as our warriors do when they have won a victory over our enemies. Then we took the dead man's tobacco-pouch and shield. I took the shield, a beautiful one that was painted. The other girl got the pouch. But our fathers made us return these things. Ah, how my father talked to me that time! And I needed to be talked to. My mother said that robbing the dead was not only a bad thing, a wicked thing that might bring me trouble, but that it was dangerous, because the Lacota might have died with the bad-sickness [smallpox]. I knew better than this. I had seen the hole that a bullet had made in the Lacota's head.

" 'You and your friend, Beaver-that-passes, will come to a bad end if you keep doing these crazy things,' my mother told me, looking frightened. But we didn't. We did pretty well. There was nothing bad about us. We loved fun, and did not let our hearts grow old too soon. Of course," she added, soberly, "this made people notice us more."

I did not doubt that Pretty-shield had always "made people notice" her. Her ready wit and contagious laugh would anywhere insure "notice." Usually Indians, men or women, who possess as little knowledge of English as does Pretty-shield, will avoid even an answer to a question asked in that language. Not so with Pretty-shield. A few days before this, when she was calling at the Agency office, a friendly employee there greeted her, "Hello, old girl." Pretty-shield, her eyes twinkling, instantly made merriment at the expense of the white man. "Allo hol' *boy!*" she replied, turning her back. She understands a little English, of the pidgin kind, and even though she knows how funny her own English sounds to others she is not averse to using it when talking, or attempting to talk, to a white friend. She is an excellent sign-talker, much too deft for me.

"Being separated from my mother, I imagined her an ideal woman, one who had no bad habits, no faults. And yet, because I saw her every day, I copied another woman in everything she did. I will tell you about her. She was the only woman of Long-horse, our great chief. Her name was Kills-good, a tall handsome woman with a soft voice. I could not make my face look like hers; but I trained my voice until it sounded much as hers did. Her own children were fine in every way, and her man, Long-horse, was happy. I could see this, and was determined to make my man happy when he took me, by being like Kills-good.

"She had a daughter named Good-cat-tails who was of the same age as myself. We were good friends, this girl and I. This gave me opportunities to visit in the lodge of Long-horse where everything was always neat. Its poles were taller, its lodge-skin whiter and cleaner, its lining, beautifully painted, reaching all around it. Its back-rests, three of them, were made with head-and-tail robes; and always Kills-good burned a little sweet-grass, or sweet-sage, so that her lodge smelled nice. She, herself, wore dresses that fitted her form. They were always neat and clean, even after a long move, and they were beautifully made. And her hair! Never while she was Long-horse's woman did I see her hair when it was not neatly braided. Long-horse kept it looking as though it had just been combed. One could always tell when a man loved his woman by her hair."

Men did their own, and their women's hair. The comb used by all the tribes of the Northwestern plains was the tail of a porcupine.

"Her daughter, too, was neater and better dressed than the other girls, and this was not because Long-horse was richer than other men, but because Kills-good was that kind of a woman. Why, even the stilts that Good-cat-tails walked on when we played were finer than those of any other girl in the tribe. I never saw the beds in Long-horse's lodge when they did not look neat; and I went often to that lodge, sometimes early in the morning. Each bed, three of them, was covered with a robe that anybody would notice.

"Yes, and the shoulder-blades of buffalo that Kills-good used for dishes were bleached snow white, and always she placed a little square of rawhide under each of them when she gave meat to anybody. Many, many times I ate with my friend Good-cat-tails in the lodge of Long-horse and his woman, Kills-good, who be-longed to the clan of The-newly-made-lodges. My aunt and my mother already had iron cups that had

33

been made by white men, but Kills-good used only the horns of mountain-sheep for drinking cups, just as her mother had.

"How I loved to watch Kills-good pack her things to move camp. The painting on her parfleches was brighter, her bags whiter, than those of any other Crow woman; and, ah, she had so many pretty things. Besides, I thought her favorite horse, a proud pinto, was far and away the best horse in the Crow tribe. And yet Kills-good was not proud. Instead, she was kindly and so soft-spoken that all the people loved her.

"But her man, Long-horse, was a proud person. He often said things to others, things that stung like the lash of a whip. I once heard Kills-good tell Long-horse that he had hurt another man's feelings, and that this was all wrong. He, our head chief, listened without saying a sharp thing to her, because she was so sure of herself, so kind to others. I tried hard to be like her, even after I grew up and had children of my own.

"After Long-horse, our chief, was killed by Lacota many men wanted Kills-good, and finally she married again. But this man was not good to her. She left him, and died single. I mourned for her as though she had been my own mother.

"It was a sad day for us all when Long-horse was

killed. I remember it as though it were yesterday. I was yet a young girl. My oldest sister had made me a kicking-ball. You have seen them. The thin skin that is over a buffalo's heart is taken off and stuffed with antelope hair. My ball was a very fine one, painted red and blue. I was so proud of this ball that I carried it, and my doll, in my robe on my back. But one day several of us girls and a boy were going to have a play sun-dance, so I left my things in camp. Our lodges were pitched on Spotted-fish creek [Judith country], a nice place for us children to play. The day was warm. Flowers were everywhere, and birds were singing in the bushes and trees. There is a cliff not far from where the Crow lodges were pitched that day, and we children pitched our brush-lodge for our play sun-dance at the foot of this cliff. We believed that our dance was real. We felt very serious. I said that there was but one boy with us. There were two, one to beat the drum, and one who danced. The dancer wore only his moccasins and breech-clout, as men do, and of course he was painted. We girls wore our usual clothes, as dancing women do, painting our faces to please ourselves.

"The dance made us forget everything else. I forgot even my ball and my doll. The beating drum, our whistles, made from the big bone of an eagle's wing, our dancing, made us grownups whose hearts were in the sun-dance. Our heads thrown back, our eyes on the sky above us, we kept our bodies going with the steadily beating drum until the dancing boy, who was next to me, stopped so suddenly that he bumped against my shoulder, his eyes filled with fright.

"Then the drum stopped; and the dancing stopped as though it had been a lodge-fire that had been put out with a kettle of water. The boy, the dancer next to me, seemed frozen to the ground. I looked up to see what held his eyes; and then my legs lost their strength. A Lacota war-party was looking down at us from the top of the cliff!

"My doll and my ball! The Lacota would get them! These were my first thoughts when my heart began beating again. I ran. We *all* ran, like a lot of frightened young sage-hens. The way was down-hill to the lodges, and our steps were long. A man with some horses was coming toward us from the village. 'Lacota! Lacota!'

"The man rode up and stopped us, laughed at us, made us say 'Lacota' again, while he looked into our eyes to see if we were lying.

"My running had taken away a little of my fear. My head was clearer now. I raced to my little lodge, caught up my doll and ball to save them from the

Lacota. My aunt called. Ho! I did not stop. There was shooting by this time, and arrows were coming, too. I ran fast, my doll and my ball in my calf-skin robe, until an old woman sprang out of a lodge and grabbed me."

Pretty-shield stopped here, brushing her eyes with both hands, as though wiping away the years.

"The old woman's face was covered with dried blood from wounds she had made upon her head while mourning for her son who had lately been killed in a battle," she went on. "There were three men, five women, and three children in this old woman's lodge, all of them mourning. The old woman held me, trying to take away my things, while the others, all with bloody faces that looked awful, talked to me, urging me to let the old woman hide my ball and doll for me; and at last I did this. But when I got the ball back again, after the fighting, it had rolled into Spotted-fish creek, and was all wet. It was soaked and sad-looking. Its beauty was gone. My heart was on the ground until my aunt made my ball pretty again. My doll could not roll, you see. It stayed where the old woman put it.

"I have taken much more time to tell you about my running away with my doll and my ball than I spent at the thing itself. A little girl's feet are fast when she is afraid. But my head was strong that day, even though my heart tried to smother me when I looked up at the top of that cliff on Spotted-fish creek.

"Our warriors drove the Lacota away. But in the fighting Long-horse was killed. His body was brought back to us, and we mourned, all of us, even I who was yet too young to understand what it all meant. We fasted, nearly starved in our sorrow for the loss of Long-horse. And of course my girl-friend, Good-cat-tails, his daughter, looked to me for sympathy. I could do but little for his woman, Kills-good. She was a strong-hearted person and could heal her own wounds.

"I cannot tell you about the fighting itself. That is a man's business. Our men were always fighting our enemies, who greatly outnumbered us. Always there was some man missing, somebody for us women to be sorry for.

"Just after the fight that started on Spotted-fish creek we moved to where the city of Billings stands today. Here we learned that the Mountain Crows had been attacked by Lacota and Cheyenne, and that three men had been killed. I knew these three men very well. One of them, an old man, was blind. It was in this camp that I first felt the sadness that comes to grown-up people with the death of a friend. The old blind man had been my friend. I had loved him much more than I had realized, and now when news of his death reached me, I wept with deeper feeling than I had ever before known."

Pretty-shield stopped talking to look at the sun. "I must go to my place now, Sign-talker," she said, wrapping her blanket around her. "My grandchildren will be hungry. I will come again in the morning."

I knew her "place," a bare shack where she and nine grandchildren slept upon the floor. "Stop at the Trader's store," I said, giving her four silver dollars.

"You pet [you bet]," she laughed, in her pidgin English. How much I wished that I could speak Crow!

THREE

"TELL me about your father and mother, Pretty-shield," I said when we met again the next morning.

"I have wanted you to ask me to do this," she said, happily. "I was thirty-two years old when my good mother died. She was not much older than I am when she went away from us. I missed her more than you can understand. My mother appeared to be well and strong as ever; and then one day when our village was on the Little Bighorn, she left us. I remember that the sun was very hot, and that our lodge-skins were

lifted and propped from the ground, so that whatever little wind came along it might pass under them. But even these little winds were hot.

"A party of us, men and women, went from our village to the hills. Before we started, my father who went with us asked my mother to water his horses during the day. My mother remembered this, and in the afternoon went out to get on a horse that had been staked near the lodge. This horse, for some strange reason, was afraid of my mother. He snorted, backed up, pulling his stake, and then ran away, dragging his rope. My mother ran after him, tried to head him back before he reached the pony-band; but she stumbled and fell down. When she got up to go on, a man who had caught the horse handed her the rope. When she took it she saw not only one man, but two. Both were her sons, my brothers, who had been killed in war. She watered my father's horses, and then went into her lodge to wait for us to return from the hills.

"Upon our return she told us what had happened. 'I am going to The-beyond-country now,' she said. 'My sons have come to take me there.' Then she laid down on her robe, and went away, sleeping."

Pretty-shield's voice was so low that I could scarcely hear it. I feared that she might not go on. But in a moment she shook off her depression.

"My father was a kind man," she said, brightening, "kind to everybody except our enemies. Toward them his heart was always bad. His medicine was the long-legged owl that lives with the prairie-dogs, and it was powerful. Yes, my father's heart was always bad toward our enemies, and yet he was kindly," she said again, as though she liked to remember him in this light.

"He was a small man, not as tall as I am," she went on, gently. "He was never known to ride past a man who was afoot, or a man on a tired horse. He belonged to The-war-clubs [a secret society].

"I am hiding nothing from you, Sign-talker," she said seriously. "My father had one bad fault that we knew about. He liked other women besides my mother pretty well; and yet he was always kindly, never cross. His heart was big.

"And even though my father was a small man he was a great warrior. He looked like his medicine, the long-legged owl that lives with the prairie dogs. The Lacota and Cheyenne and Arapahoe came often to bother us. Many times they came together, so that they greatly outnumbered us. Our men were constantly fighting. They *had* to fight. Ahh, how our men *did* fight to hold our country against our enemies; and there were so many enemies of the Crows.

"Once when the Lacota and Cheyenne came together against us our village was on Arrow [Pryor] creek. They were five to our one. There seemed to be little chance for the Crows, when my father rode through the village on a gray horse. He had stripped, and painted his face and body yellow. Zigzagging through the yellow paint, lengthwise, there were shivery lines that were like those one sees dancing over hot fires on the plains when the air is clear. These lines made it difficult to see my father, who was singing his medicine-song: 'I am the bird among the prairie-dogs.'

"He gave the Crow war-cry, and then, armed with only his medicine, the stuffed skin of the long-legged owl, tied on his head, and his coup-stick, he rode out alone against the enemy. So strong was his medicine that the Lacota and Cheyenne could not stand against him. They opened, scattered, and then the Crows were upon them, winning a great victory, because of my father's medicine, the long-legged owl that lives with the prairie-dogs.

"There were several women with the enemy that time," she went on. "When the Lacota scattered and ran away one of the women fell off her horse. My father captured her, giving her, as a slave, to his brother-in-law, Warm-robe. This woman's Crow name was Good-trader. She lived with Warm-robe and his woman and learned to love them. I liked this slave-woman very much. When she had a chance to get a man of her own she would not go with him until Warm-robe said 'yes.' It was One-leg, a good man, who took Good-trader as his woman; and they had several children. Finally, when there came peace between the Lacota and the Crows, Good-trader's Lacota man came here to get her. But she would not listen to him now," Pretty-shield chuckled. "She said, 'Look at *my* lodge, and then think of your *own*. Go away from here.' I remember how glad I felt when Good-trader spoke these words to her Lacota man. I liked her even more when I heard them.

"My father was very old when he died, so old," she said, "that his skin was cracking a little."

"Did the Lacota kill your father?"

"No. Smallpox killed him, and more than a hundred others, in one moon," she said. "I had it myself. A wise-one named Sharp-shin healed me. I believe that, if he had been asked, he might have saved others.

"This bad-sickness came to us from the Shoshones. We were in our winter camp when it came. We did not know what sickness it was. We did not scatter, as we ought to have done, and the bad-sickness got into every lodge before we knew its power. My people became terrified and died. I was not yet seventeen years old, just married. Tst, tst, tst, my heart was on the ground with many others.

"Until the bad-sickness came to our world my people were scarcely ever sick. War and accidents took many lives. We were used to these, expecting to have to meet them any day, but the bad-sickness was new, and terrible. I will not try to tell you how awful it was. When a woman sees whole families wiped out, even whole clans, and cannot help, cannot even hope, her heart falls down and she wishes that she could die. I am going to leave this now. I do not like to think about it."

45

FOUR

"WHEN did you first see white men?" I asked. "When I was six snows old," she answered, promptly. "These white men, trappers, with many pack-horses, came to our village. At first my people did not call the white man *Masta-cheeda* [yellow-eyes] as they now do. Our first name for the white man was *Beta-awk-a-wah-cha* [Sits-on-the-water] because my people first saw the white man in a canoe on Big river. The canoe was far off. The white man in it looked as though he sat on the water; and so my people named him, and his tribe. But this has now been changed, as *Maja-hah-wathus* has been changed, since I was a little girl, to *Ah-badt-daht-deah*."

Here Goes-together had trouble in translating the early Crow name for the All High, *Maja-hah-wathus*, into English. She insisted that it was "One-man." But upon asking Pretty-shield for His sign-name she answered "Man-alone," or "Alone-man," which I thought much better.

"I am sorry that my people did not know how to write," Pretty-shield said after this discussion. "All we had was our memories. I belong to the great Crow clan, a clan that has furnished many chiefs and head-men, so that I have tried to remember what happened since I came onto this world, and even what my grandmother told me.

"The three white trappers wore beards that did not look nice. And yet one of those men had kindly eyes, I remember. I saw a little girl shake hands with him. There was white in this one's beard, I noticed. All the others' were brown. I hid myself and watched the three go into the lodge of our chief, Walks-with-the-moon. I did not see inside, nor hear what was said in the lodge of Walks-with-the-moon, and yet I know that the three white men gave the Chief some tobacco, and that they smoked with him, saying that they had traveled a long time looking for the Crows. My mother told me that these white men had asked if they might stay with our people, and that Walks-with-the-moon had answered 'No,' giving them a night and a day to rest before going away. When, the next morn-ing, I looked to see the white man with the kindly eyes he was gone. I never saw him again.

"Later, when I was eleven years old, three other men who wore beards, but who were not white men, came to our people. These three caused trouble. I do not remember what it was that they did to make my people angry; but I know that two of them were killed. The other one lived for a long time with our people."

This may have been the mulatto, Jim Beckwith, or James P. Beckwourth, as he styled himself, who wore a scraggy beard. Beckwith lived with the Crows for a number of years, and was said to have been a petty chief among them. However, he must have terminated this tribal relationship before Pretty-shield was born, certainly before she was eleven years old, since he is known to have been living in Colorado in the '50s and '60s. Nevertheless there is reason to believe that he paid visits to the Crows even after he removed himself to Colorado. It is of record that in 1866 he returned to the Crow village as an envoy of General Carrington, and that he died there. The other two "who wore beards, but who were not white men," leave one groping. Robert Meldrum, a white man, had lived with the Crows, but had left them before Pretty-shield was born.

This puzzling mention of the men "who wore beards, but who were not white men," caused her to ask, "Did you ever hear that a tribe of very large people once lived on this world, Sign-talker?"

"No," I answered.

"Well, once when I was a girl, and our village was at The-place-where-we-eat-bear-meat [near the present Headgate] several of us girls walked up to The-dry-cliff. This was, to me, a strange place. A great herd of buffalo had some time been driven over the cliff, and killed by the fall to the rocks below. There were many, many bones there that told a bad story. And on top, stretching out onto the plains, there were long lines of stones in this shape [she made a V with her hands] with the narrow part at the cliff's edge. These had helped to lead the running buffalo over the cliff. I have heard old women tell of such things being done before the horse came to the plains; and yet this herd of buffalo that went over The-dry-cliff may have been driven to death by another people.

"The cliff was high, sloping in a little from the top. At its bottom were the bones, many, many bones. I noticed a dark streak on the face of the cliff. It was narrow and straight, reaching from the bottom of the cliff to the rim above. It looked to me as though the smoke of a fire that had burned there for many snows had made this dark streak on the smooth stone, and yet I had never heard anybody mention this. I could not keep my eyes from looking at this dark streak as we girls were walking toward it.

"We had brought some pemmican, and I had my

ball with me, because we intended to stay all day. The sun was past the middle when we began to dig with a root-digger at the bottom of the cliff. We were not looking for any particular thing. We were only playing. But our playing stopped suddenly when, in digging, we brought up a man's skull that was twice as large as that of any living man; and with it there were neck-bones that were larger around than a man's wrist.

"We ran away from that place, and I was first to run. The size of the skull frightened me. Upon reaching our village I told my father what we had found. He said that he wanted to see the skull. We took him to the place, sitting off quite a distance while my father smoked with the skull. He said that it was a medicine-skull, and powerful. While we girls watched him my father wrapped the great skull in a buffalo robe and buried it.

"It was Shows-the-lizard who dug up that skull; and we found the blackened sticks of an old fire there, too. Yes," she said, thoughtfully, "I believe that another kind of people once lived on this world before we came here. This big skull was not at all like our skulls. Even though I did not stay there very long I noticed that its seam ran from front to back, straight, with no divisions.

"And Shows-the-lizard, who dug up that skull, and seemed not to be afraid of it, afterward did what I thought was a rather cowardly thing," she went on, a little severely. "This happened after she and I were married women and had children, and yet we played together as we always had when we were girls. I will tell you about it.

"Our village was at the same place, The-place-where-we-eat-bear-meat. It was a winter camp, so that all our lodges were new, excepting those of a lazy woman or two. And it was a pretty village with its big circle of white lodges, all their smokes riding away on the winds.

"Snow came late that winter, I remember. We girls had always liked to slide down hill on sleds of buffalo briskets, made to stay in shape with the strong cords from the necks of buffalo. These sleds, made comfortable with a buffalo robe to sit on, would go very fast on crusted snow, even when new. After they had been used a little they could beat the North wind going down a hill. And," she chuckled, "sometimes we fell off."

Her chuckling grew into merry laughter, till turning to Goes-together she hastily recounted such a fall, speaking, without signs, in Crow. By this, and the merriment of both women, I guessed that these details were not for me.

"That didn't amount to anything," said Pretty-shield, again serious. "It was just a woman's joke. Now I will go on with my story.

"Six of us young women were sliding down a hill that was a long way from the village. Shows-the-lizard, who is yet living, was one of our sliding-party. She had a little girl with her, and so had I. We were having great fun with our sleds when I saw a man that I thought was one of our wolves signal 'The enemy is coming. Look out for yourselves.'

"I called to the others; and we ran, leaving our sleds where they happened to be, some of them on top of the hill, ready to go down, and some at the bottom. Shows-the-lizard and I, each with a little girl in our arms, ran with the others until we reached a band of horses. The other girls, who were ahead, had already caught several of these horses, and because Shows-the-lizard and I carried children they gave us each a horse. In no time we were all riding as fast as our horses could go, but far apart.

"Shows-the-lizard let the little girl fall from her arms, somehow, and yet did not stop her horse. She rode on as though nothing had happened until she learned that the signal that had caused all the trouble had been a mistake, that the wolf had seen some white trappers coming with many horses, far off on the whitened plains, mistaking them for Lacota.

"The little girl's head was wounded by the fall to the frozen ground, because she happened to fall where there were rocks sticking up. After this happened I did not feel so much ashamed of having been afraid of the big skull.

"There were strange things in the Crow country like that big skull, that told of people who came before us," Pretty-shield went on. "Once on a trip in the mountains, one of the men, Three-wolves, took the rest of us to a place where he had found a round pile of red-stone arrow-points. I never have seen so many pretty arrow-points as were there. Some were very long and slim, and there were many, many tiny ones, and all of them red. The pile was round, and this tall." She indicated about fourteen inches.

"Did you take those arrow-points?" I asked her.

"No, no," she answered, as though surprised at my question. "We never touch such things. Some *Person* [sprite] had put them there. It was a medicine-pile."

"Did you never pick up the stone arrow-points that you found on the plains and in the mountains?" I asked.

"Yes, always, when they were alone," she said. "But

53

they get lost after a time. It is strange how they leave us."

"Who made the stone arrow-points?" I asked, as I have always done whenever opportunity offered.

"There are two stories," she said. "I suppose that you know them both. But I believe the stone arrow-points that are everywhere came from Red-woman, the first woman, who was a very bad *person*. Her bones were stone. Long, long before the horse came to us, our people caught Red-woman and tried to burn her. But when the fire had burned away her flesh and her stone bones were very hot, a rain came. This rain, falling upon the hot stone bones made chips fly in all directions over the world. These chips are the stone arrow-points that are everywhere. Some of our old men say that these arrow-points were made by The-little-people who live in Medicine-rock; and they may be right. I do not know which story is the true one. One of them must be a lie," she finished, thoughtfully.

"Yes," she went on, "Red-woman was a bad *person*, and yet she was the first woman to live on this world. I do not believe that she ever had a beginning, as we do. I think she was always on the world, and that like E-sahca-wata [Old-man-coyote] she did much harm and very little good. I believe that she was finally drowned, as you shall see, and that this is the reason why nobody has seen her during my lifetime. I have already told you that once my people caught her and tried to burn her. But the fire that chipped her bones when the rain fell upon them while they were very hot, did not kill her. She was afterward seen, and was finally captured a second time by my people; and this time she was drowned. I ought to tell you that there are those among us who believe that Red-woman is yet alive and on this world. But I don't. I am certain that she was drowned. Shall I tell you the story? There is a man in it, or a boy who had the heart of a man."

"Yes," I said, beginning to fear that my repeated admonition to tell only a woman's story had prevented Pretty-shield from telling many of her own adventures.

"Well, once," she began, after settling herself upon her folded blanket, "once in early springtime, just when the chickadee began to say 'summer's near,' my people were hunting deer in the mountains. The Crows were then very poor. They had no horses. Only dogs dragged their travois and of course everybody had to work hard to make a living. It required strong arms and wrists to handle bows and arrows, so that without a man, a woman could scarcely get along.

"At the time that I am telling you about, a widow woman, with a young son who was only beginning to handle a strong bow, went with the others to hunt deer in the mountains. This boy, knowing that he was not yet an able hunter, followed the men, gathering up whatever meat they left for him, until he had all he could carry. This he made into a pack, and was about to lift it to his back when a woman appeared.

" 'Wait, my son,' she said. 'Your pack is too heavy for one so young. I will help you.'

"Before the boy could even speak a word the woman lifted the pack to her own back, and carried it to the widow woman's camp, or near it, where she let it fall to the ground. 'First you must eat,' she said, turning to smile at the boy; 'then I wish you would walk up to the foot of that cliff.' She pointed. 'I wish to talk to you there. I have something important to tell you.'

"She was tall and strong and good-looking. Besides, she had helped the boy. 'Good!' he said, 'I will do as you wish.'

"After eating, the boy told his mother that a woman wished to talk to him, and went out of the lodge. When he reached the foot of the cliff he saw the woman standing at the edge of the forest, farther away. She beckoned and smiled kindly.

"The boy started toward her but stopped, because as soon as he began to walk to her she began moving farther away, among the trees.

"When she saw that the boy was not coming the woman waited, beckoning and smiling; and this went on until at last the boy was beside her in the dark forest. A thin cloud was among the trees, the air damp and cold.

" 'Let me see your arrows,' she said, her eyes warm and kindly looking. 'Four,' she counted, handing them back. But now one was red, one blue, one yellow, and one black. She had painted them [made them medicine-arrows, magical].

"Standing behind the boy, she said: 'Shoot one of your arrows as far as you can in that direction.' She pointed, and the boy let an arrow go. He could see nothing ahead of him. The thin cloud was everywhere. But now, after his arrow had gone from his bow-string, he felt colder. The cloud that was everywhere looked heavier.

" 'Ahhh! Your arm is strong,' said the woman's voice behind him. 'Shoot another arrow in the same direction. You will not lose it. I will find it for you.'

"She had made him feel proud. He let another arrow go; and in no time the white cloud around them was so heavy that he could not even see the woman. He shivered with cold, and two wolves howled.

" 'Your wrist is powerful,' whispered the woman, her mouth near the boy's ear. 'I have never before seen such strength in a young man's wrist and arm. Shoot another. You will not lose it.'

"Another, the third arrow, flew away. Almost at the twang of his bow-string the boy felt warmer. The cloud was again thin, thinner than it had been when he first noticed it. He could see the trees plainly now, could even count them, and yet he did not know what trees they were.

"'Ahh, a grown-up man, a warrior who has counted coup, would be proud of such arms and wrists as you have. Now let the other arrow go, my son. I will watch where it falls.'

"The woman's words made the boy's heart jump. The fourth arrow, the black one, cut a hole in the thin white cloud; and then the boy was standing by the door of a tall, white lodge in a strange country. The cloud was gone. Bright sunlight that was soft warmed his body. Birds were singing, but he had never before heard their songs. Flowers were there, and tall trees, and yet both were strange. He did not know them, did not know the country, could not even guess where he was. Thoughts of his mother made his heart fall down to the ground.

"'Here are your arrows, all of them, my son.' The woman's voice startled him. 'Take them,' said the woman, lifting up the lodge-door. 'This is our camp, yours and mine, my son. Come in. We will eat fat meat, and then rest awhile.'

"Leaving his arrows outside, the boy followed the woman into the lodge; and never before was there such a lodge as this one. It was rich in all ways, and large. The boy could not believe that there could be such a lodge; and there was plenty of fat meat. Strange marks and pictures in bright colors were thick on the lodge-skin, and not one of them did the boy know.

" 'There is your robe. Sleep,' said the woman, after they had eaten.

"When the boy wakened, and sat up, wondering where he was, the woman said: 'My son, you are very far from your country. You would die of old age, even though you walked day and night, before you reached it. Besides this, my medicine is strong. You cannot get away from me. Do as I tell you, and you will be happy here. Disobey me, and you will be sorry. Go now and kill a fat buffalo calf. You will have no trouble in finding a fat one. When you have killed and dressed it nicely, bring it here to me, all of it.'

"Of course the boy knew by this time that the woman's medicine was powerful. He did not intend to try to run away, so that when he found a fat calf he killed it easily, wondering at the strength of his arm and wrist. The sun being now in the middle of the sky, the boy felt hungry. While dressing the calf he took out and ate one of its kidneys, as our people often did. While he was eating the kidney a coyote came to him. Sitting down near by the coyote said: 'Brother, I am hungry. Let me have the entrails of this calf, will you?'

" 'Yes, of course,' said the boy, moving over a little to make room for the coyote.

" 'Say, brother,' said the coyote, after he had eaten, 'do you know whom you are living with?'

" 'No,' answered the boy, being afraid to say anything.

" 'Well, I'll tell you,' said the coyote, licking his lips. 'That person is Red-woman. You are in danger. Everybody is afraid of her, everybody but myself; and even I am, too, a little. But I will help you, brother,' he finished, picking up a scrap that he had overlooked.

"The boy made a pack of the calf, and started back to the woman's lodge, very much afraid now.

" 'I'll see you soon. I'll tell everybody about this,' called the coyote, looking around to see if anything was left.

"The woman missed the kidney that the boy had eaten. She was angry, and scolded him about it. When the boy told her he had eaten it because he was hungry she said, 'I'll eat *you* if you ever get fat enough. Go out now and gather some dry wood for our fire.'

"When the boy brought a back-load of wood the woman stuck out her foot, held it just where the wood would fall when the boy dropped it. 'Don't dare to let a piece of your wood strike my foot,' she said, trying to start a quarrel.

" 'Hit her foot! Hit it hard! Do it!' The coyote was standing behind the boy. His words were fast. 'Do it!' he said; and the boy let his load of wood fall. Swow!

" 'Ho-ho!' The woman began to cry. 'I'll fix you for this; I'll fix you for this,' she whined.

" 'Don't be afraid of her,' whispered the coyote. 'We are all going to help you, even the ones who are afraid of Red-woman. Now listen; when you get a chance, steal her two feathers. You'll find one on a pole at the head of the lodge, and the other on a pole by the door, just above the door. Do not burn them. Burning does no good. Tie them to a stone, and throw the stone, with the two feathers, into a deep river. This will be the end of Red-woman.'

"The coyote raised up, 'The two feathers are her *heart*,' he whispered in the boy's ear. 'Be careful. Wait until she sleeps soundly, and then steal her two feathers.'

"The boy had not noticed the two feathers, and yet

he knew that they were there in the lodge, and exactly where the coyote had said. A wind was blowing, the wind that comes when the sun is down to the world, and the sky is red in the west, when the boy lifted the lodge-door and entered.

"Red-woman, pretending that her anger had followed the sun from the world, was eating fat meat. 'Eat, and then sleep, my son,' she said, between mouthfuls. 'Eat much, and sleep well.'

"The boy, not daring to look around for the two feathers, began to eat slowly, a little mouthful at a time. At last, as though full, he laid down on his robe, pretending to sleep soundly. But all the time he kept his eyes a little open, just enough to let them watch Red-woman, who finally slept.

"The boy sat up, listening. He heard footsteps outside, soft footsteps that stopped by the lodge-door. He looked carefully at Red-woman, saw her bosom rise and fall regularly, heard her breathing deeply, saw, in the weakened firelight, that her eyes were closed, and yet he dared not move, because he knew that some person was at the lodge-door.

"The dying fire made shadows dart, reach up on the lodge-wall like yellow tongues licking a bone. It would soon be dead, and then how could the boy find the two feathers? He tore his eyes away from Red-woman's face, away from the licking shadows, to look at the door. Ho! A long nose, and two yellow eyes were there, two yellow eyes that looked like yellow fire.

" 'What are you waiting for?' whispered a voice. 'She's sleeping. Now is your time to steal her two feathers. One is on a lodge-pole over *her* head, and the other is on a pole over *my* head. Get *hers* first.'

"The boy got up. He saw the feather of a magpie over the head of Red-woman. A yellow tongue of fire-light was licking it. He would have to step over Red-woman's body to reach the feather.

" 'Hurry, because I've got to go about my own business,' said the whispering voice at the door.

"The boy stepped carefully over Red-woman, got the feather, crossed to the door, got the other one, and went out of the lodge. The coyote had gone about his own business. The boy was alone.

"But he had his medicine-arrows. Swiftly fitting them to his bow-string he shot them all toward his own country, one, two, three, four, the black arrow last. And now he was back in the land of the Crows.

"He saw his own mother standing beside a deep river, heard her call, 'Hurry! Hurry! Cross this water, my son. She is just behind you. Here, walk across on *this*.' His mother laid her medicine-root-digger from shore to shore, and the boy ran across it, to her side. And now, remembering, he tied the two magpie feathers to a stone, and threw the stone into the deep water.

"Red-woman, racing fast, reached the deep river, saw the boy and his mother beyond it, saw the medicine-root-digger reaching from shore to shore, and leaped upon it. But when she was out on its middle the boy's mother gave her root-digger a *twist*. Swow! That was the last of Red-woman. Anyhow she has never been seen from that day to this that I know of."

FIVE

"AN old Crow woman, named Plainly-painted, came to see me at my place last night, Sign-talker," said Pretty-shield next morning when she sat down in her chair beside the table. "I told her what I was doing, and she asked me if I had told you about the time we lost the baby. And then how we did laugh! But there was no laughing on the day when the thing happened; there were tears, but no laughing. I was never so much ashamed of myself as then. Tst, tst, tst! I was a long time getting over my shame.

"To me a doll was nice to play with, but a real baby was better. Even before I married I adopted a baby girl whose father and mother had been killed. I raised this child, and today she has grandchildren of her own. This love for babies made me, and some of my girl friends, a lot of trouble one day. It came about in this way:

"It was summer. Berries were turning red on the bushes. Our big village was moving. Long strings of travois and pack-horses were raising dust on the plains. I, with some other girls, among them Plainly-painted, the old woman who came to my place last night, was quite a way behind the moving village, even behind the pony bands. We were racing our horses, singing and playing. We even stopped to swim in a creek that we crossed. It was here that a woman who had been delayed, for some reason, caught up with us. She was leading a pack-horse, and on the pack there was a little child, a girl not over two years old. The woman stopped at the creek to let her horses drink. I saw that she was in a great hurry to catch up with the travois, so I said, 'Let us girls take care of your baby. We will be kind to it, and bring it safely to your lodge when the people make camp.'

"'Tst, tst, tst! I do not know what made that woman so foolish. I know that I was surprised, besides feeling glad, when she agreed, handing me the pack-horse's rope. Then away she went in a big dust, riding fast. She was out of sight by the time we girls were dressed again and ready to play with the baby.

"Of course we quarreled over it a little. Each of us wanted to mother it first; and we all did, in turn, feeling very happy with the little child until we happened to remember that all this playing was letting the moving village get farther and farther away.

"The sun was already near to the ground when I spoke of the long way ahead of us, making quite a stir among the other girls. There were always Lacota and buffalo herds to look out for, you see. We thought that we had better stop playing with the baby and catch up with our people; so we tied the baby, in its back-cradle, to the pack and started, riding moderately at first. I do not now remember who was to blame, but anyhow it wasn't long before we were racing our horses. I could scarcely keep the others in sight, because I was leading the pack-horse that carried the child. At first I kept looking back, until my neck ached, to see if the baby was there, and all right; but when the racing started I forgot this for a long time. Then, when I suddenly remembered, and looked back at the pack, the baby wasn't there!"

Pretty-shield stood up, her face grave. "Sign-talker, I cannot make you know how quickly my heart fell to the ground, nor how loudly I cried out, 'Stop! Stop! We have lost the baby!'

"Ahh," she sighed, sitting down again, "now there was excitement; yes, and tears. And, of course, all the girls blamed *me*; and, ah, how I blamed *myself*! I had not only asked to play with the baby, but it was I who led the pack-horse when the child fell off.

"We turned back, dizzy with fear. Buffalo were coming. A great herd, headed so that it would cross over the very tracks our horses had made, was sweeping toward us. We ourselves were in danger. But what of the little baby? If it had fallen in the way that the buffalo herd would travel it would be trampled into the dry plains, leaving scarcely a mark upon them.

" 'Hurry! Hurry!' I cried, riding hard, lashing my horse, my eyes wiping the ground. How long had we been racing? Nobody knew. Could it be this far back that we started it?

" 'Yes,' said some. 'No,' said others; and yet we rode on and on, our hearts in the dust with our horses' hoofs, our eyes watching the ground and the oncoming buffalo herd that luckily was not running, but moving slowly toward us.

"The sun was on the ground when some young men, who had been out after buffalo, met us. And, ahh, how fast we talked to them, how we begged them to help us! Our wind of words must have seemed like a spring storm to those young men, who were already warriors. Anyhow they laughed at us; and they even teased us, frightened us by saying that if the baby was dead we should all be killed for our carelessness.

"But at last, when they had said everything they could think of that might scare us, they rode away, looking for the baby, with us girls following in their dust. Their horses were fast. When the dust they had made blew away I saw the young men on a hillside, all of them sitting on their horses, in a circle. *None got down.* My heart smothered me. They must have found the little child. It must be dead, or one of those young men would have got down from his horse!

"I whipped my horse, that seemed to be standing still and not to feel my quirt. The hillside seemed to be moving away from us. But at last we reached it, our eyes sweeping the dry grass inside the circle of young men, who were again laughing. And there, face upward, and sound asleep, lay the baby, unharmed.

"We were off our horses before they stopped running. The child, awakened, began to cry. It was hungry and we had nothing to feed it. I took it in my arms. Ah, how glad I was to hold it, alive, in my arms! We started again for the village that we knew was by now set up somewhere far ahead. The women would be worrying, especially the baby's mother. Thoughts of meeting her filled me with fright. I was afraid, and glad, and sorry, and ashamed, all in one.

"Darkness had come by the time some men from the village met us. The summer night was warm, the moon bright, and yet I scarcely noticed these things now. I was too frightened. We were scolded, of course, as we ought to have been. The baby's mother said sharp things to us, especially to me, things that smarted for a long time afterward. For more than a whole snow I was afraid of that woman. Whenever I saw her coming toward me in the village I hid myself. I never again tried to borrow a baby—and I never loaned one," she added, slowly, her hands falling to her lap.

"That baby's name was Turtle," she went on, as though her thoughts were far away. "She is dead now. But her children are yet with us; and of all the girls who were with me when I lost Turtle that day, ten of us, there are but three alive."

She turned to speak to a girl of perhaps fourteen years, who had entered the room a moment before. The child was comfortably, even well dressed, and had a neat appearance. But like the boy of the other day, she wanted money, and got it.

"She is a grand-daughter of mine, a child of Pine-fire's," Pretty-shield explained, after the girl had gone. "She is of the first lot that I raised from babies. I hope that I can save my grandchildren. But times have changed so fast that they have left me behind. I do not understand these times. I am walking in the dark. Ours was a different world before the buffalo went away, and I belong to that other world.

"What shall I tell you now?" she asked, brightening by sheer will.

"Tell me what made that scar on your forehead," I suggested.

She laughed so heartily that both Goes-together and I joined her without knowing why. "I am glad you thought of that," she said, merrily. "I was feeling around for something to tell you, but my mind was like an empty bag.

"You see"—she pointed to the scar that began in the center of her forehead, and ran down to the point of her left eye, against her nose—"it was a wound that nearly took my eye.

"We were camped on Big river. It was summer, and I was seven years old. I, with two other little girls, was digging turnips, using a very sharp digger made from a limb of a chokecherry tree. The sun was hot. You have seen the heat dancing above the grass on the plains? Well, the heat was dancing that day, and even the birds were thirsty for water. It is at such times that old buffalo bulls go mad. Whipped out of the herds by the younger bulls, horned out, and kept out, they go mad. This did not often happen in the Crow country where there are so many big rivers, but eastward, in the Lacota country, old bulls often went mad during dry summers; and they were dangerous. They would charge a man on a horse, charge anything that moved on the plains, because they were crazy.

71

"We were quite a way from the lodges, these two little girls and I, busy at our root-digging. Everything was very still. There were only the women, and a few old men in the camp, and these were sitting in the shade of the lodges, too warm to even smoke. The turnips were plentiful, but hard to dig because the ground was so dry; and besides we were too little to have great strength. I had found a very large turnip and had poked my digger into the hard earth beside it, when I heard my mother calling: 'Look out, girls! Run! Run!'

"I raised up, glancing quickly over my shoulder. A big buffalo bull was coming at us, his face white with foam!

"Jerking my root-digger out of the ground, I ran. We *all* ran; but the string on my moccasin caught on a sage bush, and I fell, so that the point of my sharp root-digger stuck into my forehead, its tip in the corner of my eye.

"The men killed the bull, or I should have been ripped to strips. But I knew nothing about all this, nothing about anything that happened after I stumbled.

"A boy, a cousin of mine, tried to pull the digger out of my forehead; but when my mother saw that my eye was going to come out with it, she stopped him. I do not know when my father came to our lodge. I know that he had been out running buffalo, and that when he came in and saw what had happened he sent for Medicine-wolf, a wise-one, giving him the best war-horse he owned to try to get the stick out of my forehead without taking my eye with it. Besides this, my brother gave Medicine-wolf his best shirt and leggings.

"Medicine-wolf did not even touch the stick. He sat down and made motions with his hands, as though pulling at something. Once, twice, three times, four times, he made these pulling motions; and the root-digger came out, leaving my eye lifted a little. This he pushed back into its place with his fingers.

"But my forehead and eye swelled badly. I had a headache for nearly a moon afterward, and had to ride on a travois whenever the village moved. I got well. In three moons I was strong again; but my left eye has never been as good as it was before that mad bull got after me.

"Now I must go to my place and feed my grandchildren. When I come back I will tell you about another buffalo that nearly caught me; and this one was not a bull, but a cow."

She got up, rather stiffly, and started for the door,

limping noticeably. "Are you lame?" I asked, thinking that perhaps I might get another story.

"No, no," she laughed, turning at the door. "I am just old, Sign-talker, just an old woman. But, one day I *did* hurt my back. A bad horse threw me, hard. I thought for a time that I should never again be able to walk. And I wasn't, until one morning I said, 'I *will* walk!' And then of course I *did* walk."

"I'll *bet* you did," I thought, as she left the room with Goes-together. Watching from the door I saw that when Pretty-shield reached the Trader's store she was no longer limping. "Old age will have a tussle with *you*," I said to myself, marveling at the old Crow woman's power of will.

And then, as I went to my lunch, I thought of Goes-together, our good-natured interpreter, who could read and write English, and had even joined a church. She, a comparatively young woman of the same blood as Pretty-shield, frequently complained of her physical condition, had done this less than an hour ago. Pretty-shield, nearly twice the age of Goes-together, had remained an old-fashioned Indian, believing as her grandmother had believed. She had nothing to complain of, no affliction, excepting grandchildren; and this was an affliction of simple-hearted love.

SIX

PRETTY-SHIELD was exceptionally merry when she returned to the schoolhouse. "I am beginning to like this," she said, removing a black silk muffler from her head. "It is like looking for things in a bag. I just feel around till I find something; and I've got something now. I want to tell you about that buffalo cow that chased me," she went on, chuckling happily.

"I laugh, and you will laugh at what happened. I was a good-sized girl, almost a grown woman, and that buffalo cow made me forget all this. It was the moon when the sage-hens dance [April]. Our village of many, many lodges was not far from the land that is now covered by the city of Sheridan, Wyoming. The grass was very green on the hillsides that faced the south, and the day was so fine that I took my little sister and brother out on the plains to play. Along one side of a deep coulee there was rock that had many holes in it. These holes made fine places for play-lodges, and we found a very nice one to play with. It was not high enough even to sit in, but by stretching oneself on the ground and edging into the hole sidewise, there was room to lie down inside. The ground sloped gently down from this hole to the level plains where our lodges stood, and I could see even the dogs in the village. We were having a good time, my little sister and brother and I, when a boy, who was a little younger than I was, came to us.

" 'See that lone cow over there?' he pointed. 'Well, I have heard that if you say—' "

Here Pretty-shield stopped, thinking deeply, her clenched hand pressed against her scarred forehead.

"I have forgotten what it was that the boy said," she went on. "Anyhow, whatever it was, he told me that if the words were spoken to a lone cow she would charge the speaker. I did not believe this, and said so.

" 'Well, I'll show you,' he laughed, himself not believing what he had said, I am sure. Walking a few steps toward the cow that was not far away he shouted the words at her.

"Ahhh! The cow began to paw the ground as though the words had angered her.

"I stepped backward, took hold of my little sister and brother, afraid that the cow would charge.

"The boy, seeing this, called out those words again —and the cow *did* charge!

" 'Run! Run!' cried the boy, dashing away for the lodges.

"But how could *I* run? I wanted to run bad enough, but my little sister and brother could not run, you see. My legs trembled. They wanted to get away from that place. But my head was not trembling. I pushed my little sister and brother into the hole in the rock, my heart pounding like a dance-drum. 'Stay here. Be very still until I come back,' I said. And then I ran! Ahh, how I *did* run that day, with the angry cow just behind me gaining at every jump.

"The lodges, all looking exactly alike to me now, seemed far away. I made straight for the nearest, tumbled headlong through its door, and threw my arms about a man's neck, pushing him over backward to the ground."

She stopped to chuckle, her eyes fairly dancing. "That man thought that I had come there to love him, until the cow struck his lodge, Swow! The poles lifted from the ground; the lodge nearly turned over. The cow tore all the pegs on one side from the ground. Then I heard a shot. The cow was dead. An old man had killed her among the lodges. The fat on her back was the thickest that I have ever seen.

"The man that I hugged had been wounded. He was sitting by a little fire in his lodge, because he was yet weak from a bad wound. I can yet see the surprise that was in his eyes when I pushed him over," she laughed. "I was a good-sized girl, and yet when I plunged into that lodge I should have hugged a big white bear if he had been there instead of the man.

"That cow had four teeth in front, on her upper jaw, Sign-talker," she said, leaning toward me, across the table. "I had never seen such a thing before. There was something wrong with that cow, yes, something was wrong.

"Have the men, has Plenty-coups, the Chief, ever told you about our medicine-gun?" she asked, as though suddenly reminded of an episode.

"No," I answered.

"I am trying to tell you only a woman's story, as you wished. I am telling you my *own* story. The medicine-gun is a part of it, because I was with the boy who found the medicine-gun.

"Our village was near The-bad-mountain. It was our winter camp, so that the lodges had been there a long time when the thing happened. Winter was our time for story-telling. Old ones told of Old-man-coyote until the fires grew dim, and listeners fell asleep. Evenings were long, and there was not much excitement, because the men did not often go to war while the snow was deep. There was dancing, and we girls liked to watch the women when they danced the owl-dance. But even with the story-telling and the dancing, there was not much to make us girls merry, except our daytime playing.

"I was yet a little girl, playing with other little girls, and even little boys when they happened to be with me. One day in the fourth moon of the winter that we spent at The-bad-mountain several of us girls, and some boys, were playing along a deeply cut trail that had been made by buffalo and deepened by our own travois. This deep trail was bare of snow, and even outside it, on the ridges, the winds had blown the snow away, piling it into drifts that were frozen hard as stone.

"We had rigged travois to some dogs, and while we girls traveled the deep trail, pretending that our play-village was on the move, the boys kept out on the ridges, playing that they were our wolves. They would signal to each other and to us, as the men do when they are the wolves for the grownups. We were having a fine time.

"We had traveled a long way from the village when one of these wolf-boys, high up on a ridge that had a big snow drift on its top, called, 'Ho! Ho! I have found an enemy's gun. Ho! Ho!'

"He began to dance, holding the gun high above his head. And he sang: 'I thank you, I thank you,' over and over again, dancing in a circle, brandishing the gun.

"The other boys, filled with excitement, ran to him, each anxious to handle the gun. We girls, too, were curious, leaving our dogs with their travois in the deep trail, to climb the hill to have a look at the gun.

"It was old and rusty. Nobody but a boy would have even picked it up. It had been lost a long time. We do not know who lost it to this day. A Lacota may have dropped it, or even a Pecunnie [Piegan]. Nobody knows. Guns were not plentiful then.

"The boys, excited by having the old gun, began a war-dance on the hill, taking turns at carrying the gun, proud as men sage-hens when they dance before their women. And of course we girls formed a circle about them, ducking down whenever a boy, carrying the gun, would point it at us, and try to make the old hammer fly down. But the red rust would not let it move. It was stuck. No matter how hard they pulled its trigger the old gun would not work.

" 'Ho!' Suddenly a boy who was carrying the gun ran out of the circle; and the dance stopped. 'I'm going to load this gun,' said the boy, stopping a little way down the hillside where he pulled some leaves from a sage bush, and stuffed them into the gun's muzzle, ramming them down with the crooked ramrod. 80

" 'Now charge me, *all* of you,' he challenged the other boys. 'I can whip you, *all* of you. Come, you, if you dare!'

" 'Whoooooooo!' the other boys gave the war-cry.

" 'Wait! Wait!' The boy who had found the old gun undressed, stripping himself to his moccasins and breech-clout. 'I will charge you alone,' he called. 'I will charge you, take your weapon away from you, and count coup on you. Ho!'

" 'Come on! I am waiting. Come on, and be killed, you dog of a Lacota!' the boy called back, his gun ready.

" 'Whooooooo!' The naked boy dashed down the hill to count his coup.

"He was upon the boy with the gun when there was a red flash, a flat-sounding report, and a loud cry, all at once.

"In the brown smoke that smelled bad I saw the boy who had charged, the naked one, lying on the ground. Blood was running out of his mouth and nose.

"I ran. We *all* ran; even the boy who had fired the shot ran. But he did not run far. He went back, lifted the dying one's head, and said, 'I'm sorry. I did not mean to kill you, my friend.'

" 'I know you didn't, and yet you have killed me,'

replied the naked one. This was all he said. He never spoke again.

"The dead boy's oldest brother tied the old gun upon his own back, keeping it there day and night, during all his time of mourning. I have tried to forget all of this, and yet it stays in my mind as though I wished to keep it there.

"The old men said that it was the sage-leaves, the leaves which the boy had put into the old gun, that made it send its big round ball into the naked one's heart. They said it was a medicine-gun, or it could not have done what it did do, what I *saw* it do. The men kept it, often carried it into battles; and always when the old medicine-gun was with them they whipped the enemy. This medicine-gun is with us yet.

"I was always afraid of it, myself. And yet guns did much to make our lives easier. Our men could kill the buffalo without so much trouble after they got guns. I remember when the Big White Chief in Washington gave our men guns and powder and lead, because they were friendly toward white men. These guns strengthened us against our enemies, who were also enemies of the white men. The guns killed quickly, and I think now, a little too quickly. Looking back I can see this, and other mistakes that we made.

"It was the coming of the horse that brought the

best change of all to the Crows. This was long before my time, and yet I have heard my grandmother tell of the days when old women, too worn out and weak to travel afoot on the long drives when dogs dragged the travois, had to be left behind to die. She told me that when an old woman was used up, no good any more, the people set up a lodge for her, gave her meat, and wood for her fire, and then left her there to finally die. They could do nothing else. They could not pack old women on their backs, and dogs could not drag them. In those days when *men* grew too old to take care of themselves they dressed in their finest clothes and went to war against our enemies, often alone, until they found a chance to die fighting. Sometimes these old men went out with war-parties of young men just to find a chance to get killed while fighting. It was different with the old women. They sat in their lodges until their food was gone, until their fires were out; and then they died, alone.

"All this was changed by the horse. Even old people could ride. Ahh, I came onto a happy world. There was always fat meat, glad singing, and much dancing in our villages. Our people's hearts were then as light as breath-feathers."

The downy feathers of an eagle, or of any other bird, are called "breath-feathers." Striking an armed enemy with a bow, coup-stick, lance, or with the hand, or disarming him, without injury, counted the most honorable of coups. Killing and scalping an enemy did not entitle a warrior to count a coup.

"No, we never made bull-boats in my time," she said in answer to my question, "but our relatives, the Dirt-lodges [called by white men, Gros Ventres], did. We used rafts and horses to cross the streams. We had plenty of horses, and there were always logs along the rivers. Our men used their horses to pull rafts across big water, and there were few accidents, fewer than there might have been with bull-boats [bowl-like, skin-covered boats].

"Ahh, my people were tough in those days," she said, shaking her head. "Tst, tst, tst! Now, when people get a little wet they build a fire and get dry again. In those old days when I was young, if in winter a person fell into icy water, he got out, took off his wet clothes, and rolled in the snow, rubbing his body with it, and got warm. Then, after squeezing out the water, he put on his clothes and forgot about getting wet. Yes, and the buffalo-runners rubbed their hands with snow and sand, so that their fingers would be nimble at handling the bow and arrows. Now my people wear gloves, and too many clothes. We are soft as mud."

SEVEN

S HE had promised to bring me a little of the tribal "tobacco-seed," which each year is ceremonially planted by the Crows. I reminded her of this promise now, being anxious to have the seed identified by a competent herbalist, even though I should first have to plant the seed, and reap stalk, leaves and pods. She said that she would bring the seed when she came again to the schoolhouse.

She did not forget the "tobacco-seed," but handed me a tiny, painted, buckskin pouch as soon as we took our seats beside our table the next morning. "Do not put your fingers near your mouth after handling this seed, Sign-talker," she warned me, as I put the red pouch into my coat pocket.

I felt a little surprise at getting the seed so easily. I knew by past experiences that the Crows do not like to let it pass to others. And yet I had twice before succeeded in getting a few "tobacco-seeds" only to waste them by sending them to colleges for identification. This time I meant to plant the seed myself, and so from harvesting it, have enough to last until

I learned more about it. I know that it is said by the Crows to have been first discovered on swampy ground on a high hill between the mouth of the Rosebud and Miles city, on the south side of the Yellowstone river, and that it is said, by the Crows, to grow in no other place.

"Shall I tell you how we came by this Tobacco-seed?" asked Pretty-shield, untying the black silk muffler from her head with fingers that were as nimble as a girl's.

"Not now," I said. "I will ask you about this, and many other things by and by. Tell me more about your life as a little girl."

"Good!" she laughed. "That was a happy time on a happy world. There was always fat meat, and glad singing. And yet, of course, there were many things that did not make us laugh when they happened, even though we laugh at them now. Looking back at things that frightened me when a girl I often laugh, alone. I like to laugh. I always did. Our hearts stay young if we let them."

She stood up to fold her blanket and place it on the seat of her chair, glancing sidewise at Goes-together, who giggled.

"She is fatter than I am," smiled Pretty-shield,

sitting down upon her blanket with apparent satisfaction, "and younger," she added, playfully.

"What I am now going to tell you happened in much less time than it will take to tell it," she said. "I was moving very fast, myself, before the thing was finished, as you will see. And yet it all began slowly enough for anybody.

"The summer day was hot. You have said that I must always tell you what the weather was like, and I am doing this. The day was *hot*, so hot that our horses dripped sweat while standing beneath shady trees. Our village had been ten days on the Big river when we moved. It had been in a pleasant cottonwood grove beside the water. The country to which we were going was not nice, so that we girls, about ten of us, lingered in the pretty grove a long time after the lodges were gone. Then we rode races to catch up, the hot sun making both our horses and ourselves uncomfortably warm.

"One girl, on a fast horse, was far ahead when she stopped by a creek that we had to cross. 'Let's take a swim here,' she proposed, getting down to walk into the water with her dress on.

"It was a calico dress. Her mother had bought the cloth from a white trader. 'Come on,' she called, sitting down in the water that nearly covered her mouth.

'Don't wait to take off your clothes. We must hurry.'

"She was older than the rest of us. Perhaps she was playing a joke on us. Anyhow I walked into the water and sat down beside her, forgetting that mine was a buckskin dress, a very nice one that had many elk-teeth on it. I wish that you might have seen that dress when I came out of that creek. I undressed now, and squeezed the water out of my gown until it looked awful. Then I rubbed it dry; but it was so badly stretched that it had no shape, and looked very bad. The other girls who wore buckskin dresses did not go into the water with their clothes on, as I did, and yet they all helped me rub my dress dry.

"All this took a lot of time, and of course the moving village was getting farther away while we were swimming and rubbing my dress. When we again started to catch up we rode at a fast gait, and yet did not race our horses. One of the girls was riding a horse that carried a pack on its back. She was the youngest among us, and her horse, an old white mare, was slow. She was always behind, and I felt a little responsible for her. Knowing very well that riding on a pack is not too comfortable I, at last, waited for her.

" 'Let us change horses,' I suggested when she rode up. 'You ride mine, and I will try yours for a while.'

I did not intend to let her keep my horse all the way to the village, and yet that is the way things turned out.

"We made the change. By this time the other girls were far ahead. They had even disappeared over a high hill, so that we rode as fast as we could to catch up to them. Upon reaching the hill-top I saw the moving village, and our people still traveling east, and a great herd of buffalo coming, traveling north. The herd would cut us off from our people who, I noticed, were going to camp on account of the coming buffalo. The other girls had nearly reached the travois now, and were safe.

" 'Ride! Ride! Ride fast!' I called to the young girl on my good horse. 'Ride to the village!'

"She needed no urging. Seeing the danger she dashed away, leaving me behind, which was the only thing to do.

"A buffalo herd travels straight. Nothing turns it. This was a big herd, narrow in front, and very wide behind; and it was *running*. If I rode back, or stayed where I was, it would sweep me along with it. I saw that there was only one thing to do, and this was to ride across in front of it, as the other girls had done.

"I whipped that old white mare till my arm ached. But it did little good. She could not make it. When the big herd closed around me I did not expect to see my people again.

"The old mare turned to run with the buffalo. She *had* to; and I let go of my rope to hang onto the pack with both hands. I could hear nothing above the roar of the pounding hoofs, could see nothing in the blinding dust as the old mare, pushed this way and that way, raced on with the buffalo. I saw that they were passing us, that they were going faster than we were, but with such a herd as this one was I knew that the old mare would die long before the tail-end reached us. If she stumbled in the dust, if she stepped into a badger-hole, if she fell, we should both be trampled into bits too small for even a magpie to notice. I wondered if my rope might be dragging. If it were down, and dragging, the buffalo would surely step on it, and then we should fall. Hanging onto the pack with one hand I reached over to feel for the rope with the other, and found it, coiled in the hand that was clinging to the pack. Just as I felt a little relief at this, a big bull scraped away the mare's pack on one side. I felt my saddle turn. Leaning far over I threw my weight against it; but the other pack wanted to fall off. It was hard to hold with my body. My arms were aching. My head was dizzy. I knew that I could not hold on much longer; and just then something struck my face, something that struck hard, and then slid down in the dust.

"The old mare began to slow up, finally stopping so suddenly that I went over her head, Swow!"

Pretty-shield, speaking rapidly, with her hand on the table, was standing up. Now, as though she had been actually riding with the buffalo herd, she sat down, wearily.

"I was so frightened that I had not noticed my father who, pressing his good buffalo-horse, worked us, the old mare and me, out of the herd," she said, using her black muffler to wipe away the perspiration on her forehead. "The thing that struck my face," she went on, "was a rawhide rope. A man whose Crow name was Pecunnie roped the old white mare as soon as my father had worked her near enough to the herd's edge to be safe. She had gone crazy, and soon must have fallen down.

"My father must have been riding near me for a long time, crowding the old white mare out of the herd, while Pecunnie raced along its edge with his rope ready. My mother and sisters and brothers were glad when I reached our lodge, I can tell you," she finished, more tired than I had ever seen her.

"A crazy horse is a bad thing," she went on. "Once in the fall when the leaves were beginning to change

91

their color, we girls, playing and singing as usual, rode ahead of the line of moving travois. We were behind the warriors, and yet quite a way ahead of the women, when a girl's mother caught up with us. She asked her daughter, who was then my closest friend, to help her drive the horse-band, and of course the girl turned back to help her mother.

"The horse that my friend was riding had been gentle for a long time, and yet as soon as the girl began to help her mother with the horse-band this horse went crazy. It ran away with her, throwing her so that her foot caught in her stirrup, and she was dragged. I saw it all. I wish I hadn't. My heart fell to the ground when I saw my best friend behind that plunging, kicking horse. And the plains, just there, were covered with cactus plants. Ah, it was a bad thing, a bad thing to remember, and yet I cannot forget it.

"A man roped that crazy horse, and we stopped where we were. My friend's face and body were swelling large by the time we had a lodge pitched. We tried to pick out the cactus spines. We worked as fast as we could, but she died while we worked. This saddened me for the rest of the fall, and even into the winter."

She sat wistful a moment. Then I saw her lift her

head to listen to the clatter of a band of horses being driven past the school building.

"Have I told you about my father's buffalo-horse running away with me?" she asked, as though the passing animals had reminded her of the story.

"No," I said.

"He was a buckskin, and fast," she began, full of animation again. "My father said that there was no faster or smarter horse in the Crow tribe than this buffalo-horse of his. I think he stole him from the Lacota. He was always fat and pretty to look at. And he was so gentle that a little child was safe with him. But if once he started to run after a buffalo! Ahh, then he went wild, crazy. A strong man could not hold him when once he started after a buffalo.

"My father never rode him when the village moved, never wasted him on foolishness, so that sometimes after long rests he grew too full of life. One morning when the village was moving my father told me that I might ride his buckskin. I was but ten years old, and light on his back, you see. And yet my riding him on this day would give him something to do.

"We were moving from Rotten-grass to Lodge-grass. I felt so proud of myself that I could scarcely wait to find a couple of my girl friends, so that they might notice my father's fast buffalo-horse. Together we girls waited for the travois to move out, and then we visited, even stopping to play at kicking the ball. By the time the sun was in the middle we came upon buffalo, many of the cows having calves by their sides. I thought that I would rope one of the calves, just to show off. I made a great mistake when I headed that horse toward the herd.

"He noticed that I seemed to want a calf, and picked one out for me, a good fat one, too. I threw my rope, but missed. The buckskin kept right on after that same calf, as though no other one would do. Before I knew what was happening I was in the running herd, my horse going like the wind after that calf, dodging in and out among hundreds of buffalo cows and calves, with no thought of letting his choice get away. I dropped my rope, luckily a short one, to hold on to my saddle. I could have touched that calf with my hand, any time, but now I did not want it. Disgusted because I did not shoot, the buckskin horse struck that calf with his front hoof, knocking it down, and jumping over it to save himself from falling.

"When he did that I screamed. That's about all there is to the story. My father, wondering what could have happened to hold us so long, came back for us. He took the buckskin away from me. 'This horse has more sense than you have,' he said. 'He saw that if any meat was going to be killed he would have to do the killing himself; and then you screamed,' he laughed.

"Running buffalo was a man's business, anyhow," she said, thoughtfully. "Every time that I got mixed up with a buffalo herd I wished myself anywhere else. Good buffalo-horses always went wild when they ran after buffalo. Even old pack-horses would sometimes get foolish and think themselves buffalo-runners," she chuckled.

EIGHT

WALKING to the Sloan home where I was a guest I met Mr. C. H. Asbury, the Superintendent. "How are you getting along with Pretty-shield?" he asked, with apparent interest.

"She is doing her utmost. If I fail to get her story the fault will be my own," I told him, adding, "She is a strong character, a good woman."

"Yes, Mr. Linderman, she *is* a good woman," he said, with feeling. "I do not know how some of these people could have lived without her. She is charity

itself. She has mothered the motherless; and when at
last old Gabriel blows his horn if Pretty-shield doesn't
receive rich reward for her services here on earth
the rest of us will be out of luck, I'm afraid."

I know that nothing is so binding to an Indian of
the Northwestern plains as blood relationship, and yet
I could not help wondering at Pretty-shield's fidelity
to her grandchildren, to the memory of her man,
Goes-ahead, her children, and her clan, The-sore-lips.

When, in the morning, Pretty-shield came to the
schoolhouse she was as merry as a chickadee. Before
seating herself she walked to the window, commenting

on the sun's brightness, and on the green that the young grass was showing on the plains, as though she disliked the thought of staying indoors.

"They have some prisoners locked up in the Agency jail," she said, thoughtfully; and then, just as I reacted to what I believed were her thoughts concerning the unfortunate men who, for their misdemeanors, had been shut away from the sunlight, she said: "If the Superintendent would make these prisoners rake up the leaves that are so thick beneath these cottonwood trees, things would look a little nicer around here. And besides," she added, quite severely, "it would serve those young men just right if they were made to do a little work to pay for getting drunk on white man's whisky." Then she added, "Now what shall I tell you?"

"You told of having been adopted by your aunt, and yet you seldom tell about your living with her. Why is this, Pretty-shield?" I asked.

"Ahh, but I did live with her. I lived with my aunt nearly as much as I lived with my mother," she said, earnestly. "And when my man, Goes-ahead, took me I brought my aunt to live with us, because she was a widow. Have I not told you that she was a widow, that her man had been killed by the Lacota, Sign-talker? Of course I have; and when finally I went to live with my man there were several lodges of the Crazy-sister-in-law family all pitched together; and we got along very well. There was not a lazy one among us."

"Tell me more about your life when you were a little girl, about things you liked, and things you feared."

"The white bears [grizzlies] were bad," she said, quickly. "One of them once bit off a woman's nose. And of course there was always a Lacota to be afraid of. We girls often met the white bears in the berry patches. Sometimes women were killed by them. Our men killed but few of these big bears in my day. They were very powerful, those big white bears.

"I remember that when I was a little girl we moved our village from The-bad-mountain [head of Mussel-shell] to a creek that had but few trees along its banks. I never heard its name. Berry bushes were plentiful there, and when we reached this creek the berries were ripe. The women were going to pick them, and hurried to pitch their lodges. One woman was in such a hurry that she set up her lodge where my mother's had a right to be. This woman did not even wait to finish pegging down her lodge, but started for the berry bushes, with her bag, as though she wished to fill it before the other women had a chance at the berries.

99

"I forgot to tell you that at this time I was with my own mother, visiting her and the Mountain Crows. As soon as we reached this camp the men went out to kill buffalo, leaving only the women and children with the lodges. But always our chief sent out his wolves [scouts] to the high places to watch for enemies, so that we women felt safe enough.

"I had pitched my own little lodge, and now I asked my mother if I might not go after berries with the woman who had already disappeared among the bushes. But my mother said that I must take care of my little sister, that she would attend to the berry-picking when her lodge was made ready for the night.

"I led my little sister to my play-lodge and began to amuse her. The sun was half way down from the middle of the sky, and not yet had any, excepting the first woman, gone after berries. I could see one of our wolves on a high hill, and recognized him. His name was Crazy-brave. His medicine was the dragon-fly; and he was always painted to look like a dragon-fly.

"Suddenly I heard a scream far out among the berry bushes. I ran to my mother with my little sister, the words of the screaming woman sending thrills up my back: 'Help, Help! Bears are after me!'

"My mother made me lie down with my little sister. Then she piled robes on top of us both. I could yet hear the woman running, and screaming, even hear my mother call to Crazy-brave, the wolf I had seen on the hill; but of course I could see nothing.

" 'Bear, Bear! Help me!' The frantic woman's voice made me lie close to the ground. My little sister began to cry. I tried to sing to her, but my song would not come, because my heart was in my mouth.

"Then I heard a man's voice. It was Crazy-brave's. 'Look out for yourselves here. I will go to the woman. The bear will not see me. I am the dragon-fly,' he said; and then he began to sing his song as he walked, with a big knife in his hand, into the bushes.

"The woman was kneeling beside a bush, her head on the ground, so that her arms might save her face. The bear had torn her back terribly, and her side was ripped open. Crazy-brave walked straight to the bear that did not seem to see him. This was because he looked like a dragon-fly, and because he was singing his song. Crazy-brave did not stop walking until he drove his knife into the bear's throat.

"By this time several other men had come in, and they quickly finished the bear, who turned to fight them. When the bear charged the men the woman sprang to her feet, running to the nearest lodge, which happened to be my mother's. But she fell head-first through the door. I could stay beneath the robes no longer, and crept out, leaving my little sister sound asleep there.

"The woman, torn and bleeding, looked awful. My mother called Painted-woman, a wise-one, whose medicine was the *bear*. She came quickly. 'Get me the skin that the bear has torn from this woman's body,' she told the men, who had looked in.

"The bear had swallowed it, of course, so that the men had to open the bear's stomach to get it out. But they could not get it *all* in time. One piece, a large one, was missing. While they looked for it, the woman died. Her name was Kills-by-the-water.

"We were not far from Heart Mountain. Painted-woman said, 'My medicine tells me that there are more bears around here. If, in the morning, there is a cloud on the mountain we must move, or lose more women.'

"I was up, and outside the lodge before day came, trying to see the top of Heart Mountain. When, at last, I could see it there was a white cloud over it. We moved. Even after we had made another village far from the creek where the woman died I felt afraid. I hid my doll and my ball, often going to see if they were all right, as though they were alive and needed me.

"Now I will tell you another kind of story about

bears, one that made everybody laugh, except myself, and some other girls who were with me when the thing happened.

"I was fourteen years old. I remember my age, because I was then the same as a married woman, and had been for one year. My father had promised to give me to Goes-ahead when I became sixteen. This was the custom with the Crows. Being the same as a married woman made me try to act in a dignified manner, although I kept my girl friends and played the same as ever.

"One day in the moon when the berries begin to turn red [July] I went with five other girls to dig turnips that grew so plentifully between The-two-creeks [Davis and Thompson]. We were afoot, running races, and singing all the way to the place where the turnips grew. Then we began a race to see who could dig the most turnips, and became quiet as sleeping babies, each girl working hard to beat the others.

"I had dug a good many turnips, and stood up to rest my back, looking toward the ridges that were part of the mountains. I saw some horsemen coming. They might be Lacota. I thought they *were*. 'Lacota! Lacota!' I cried, running to a large pine tree, which I climbed. The other girls, after giving one look to the horsemen, quickly followed me, all leaving their turnips. In no time we were all up in the pine tree, among its branches, looking out at the on-coming horsemen, with our hearts beating like war-drums.

"As the horsemen raced down the hill, straight toward our tree, I saw something *under* their horses, something in the dust they were making. I could not understand this; and we were afraid now even to talk to each other.

" 'Ahh, they are *Crows!*' called one of the girls below me, on a big limb; and she laughed.

"They *were* Crows, young men who liked to play. They had roped a big white bear and two cubs, and were dragging them. These were the things that I had seen under their horses in the dust they were making.

"These young men were used to watching the country. They had seen us girls climb the tree, and now they rode straight to the pine, with their angry bears growling and scratching in every direction. 'Come down, girls! Come down and play with our little pets!' they called, looking out for themselves all the time, keeping the bears from getting too near their horses.

"When we wouldn't come down, and told them so, those young men tied their three bears to our tree, and then rode away, leaving them there. Tst, tst, tst.

"The day was so hot and still that not even a leaf

stirred. I could hear horses, away back near the village, whinnying once in a while; and birds flew over our tree but none stopped to rest in it. They saw the bears.

"Always when I looked down, and I did this all the time, that old woman-bear was looking up at *me*. I saw that she was old, that her teeth were nearly all gone, and that her heavy claws were worn out; but her eyes were bad to look at. I was afraid. We girls scarcely spoke to each other, hardly moved. The limbs that we sat on began to hurt us, and yet we were afraid even to change our positions. Of course we knew that these bears could not climb trees, that they could not get us if we stayed where we were, and yet looking down at that angry old woman-bear all the time made us all afraid.

"The sun seemed to us to have stopped traveling. I could *smell* those bears, and the smell made me feel sick. I was afraid of falling from the tree. The thought of falling down on that old woman-bear made me hang on to my limb till my fingers cramped. At last, when I was ready to cry, my father came. The young men had told the joke they had played upon us, and my father got two of the jokers to take him to our tree.

"I was stiff and sore and angry when I climbed

down. My buckskin dress was all covered with pitch. I did not speak to the two young men who had brought my father to the tree. I could have seen them suffer without feeling any pity, and I felt hurt when my father laughed. 'Why, that old bear could not bite you. She has no teeth to bite anything,' he said, as though she could not slap a person to death. It was some time before I could see anything funny in all this, but I do now. I did long ago, and have laughed a good many times.

"My father and the two young men let the old woman-bear and one cub go free. They kept the other cub to give to my aunt, who always kept a pet bear, because her medicine was the bear. She kept these bears until they were two years old, and then because they grew ugly she had them taken into the mountains and set free. I do not believe that my aunt's bears would have grown so ugly if the young men had let them alone. But they would not do this. Instead, they teased my aunt's bears, so that by the time they were two years old nobody wanted to be near them. She had them taken to the mountains every two years. I remember that when my father gave my aunt this little cub she took it in her arms, and that the little bear wiggled its ears as though it felt happy. At first she carried it in her lap when we moved camp. Then when it grew bigger it rode on top of a pack, like a baby. But finally, like the others, it got cross from being teased, and had to be sent away. But it used to follow the travois, after it grew too heavy to ride on a pack, as though it belonged to the Crow tribe, and I was sorry to see it go away.

"Cubs are like children," she went on, her blanket slipping to her waist revealing her red plaid dress of gingham. "Once after I was married, and two years after the fight on the Little Bighorn, Half-yellow-face, my uncle, took my man, Goes-ahead, and me, to look at the hole where he and the others hid while Son-of-the-morning-star and his blue soldiers were being wiped out. On this trip we went to the mountains, camping there to get bighorn and deer skins for shirts. While in the mountains I saw a thing that has made me laugh a good many times since then. It was a little thing, and yet I wish that you would write it down, because it shows that all children are much alike when they are very young.

"One day when our men were out after bighorns we women took a walk on the mountain where the trees were not too thick, and where along one side of a canyon there were steep, rocky cliffs. Looking down a long slope of grassy country that had tall trees scattered over it we saw a mother bear, a black one, digging roots for her two small cubs. She was so busy that she did not see us. And because the wind was blowing toward us she could not smell that we were there. We sat down to watch her. Anybody would have felt like laughing to see those little cubs take the roots that their mother gave them, turn about. One of the little ones was a boy, and often tried to take a root that by right belonged to his little sister. He did this so many times that his mother finally slapped him a little. But her slaps did no good. The little boy-bear tried to take the very next root that belonged to his sister. This time his mother slapped him four times, rolling him over and over down the hill. When he stopped rolling he sat up, with his little fat back toward his mother. She called him to come and get a root, but he didn't answer, did not even turn his head. He was *mad*, mad at his mother for slapping him that way. Tst, tst, tst, I could scarcely keep from laughing out loud."

Here Pretty-shield assumed an attitude of pouting, her general position so nearly like that of a bear that both Goes-together and I were convulsed with laughter.

"Ahh," she went on, her face merrier than ever, "when his mother moved on to find more roots to dig the little boy-bear did not follow her. No, he sat there looking across the canyon at a big hole in the rock, as though he had a good mind to set up a lodge for himself. We thought that he would soon be sorry and follow his mother, but he did not. He just sat there. He was *mad*. I said, 'Let us catch that little boy-bear while his mother is not with him.'

"The other women agreed. In no time at all we had him. He did not cry or bite. He was *glad*," she smiled, understandingly. "He wanted to leave his mother because she had slapped him. But she came after us. Ho! We dropped the little boy-bear, and ran as fast as we could; and this is the thing that I wanted you to write down, Sign-talker; that little boy-bear was so mad at his mother that he followed us until his mother caught him, and slapped him back, the way she wished him to go. He acted exactly like a naughty Crow boy, that little boy-bear did. He believed he wanted to live with us. I never forgot this.

"It was I who lifted the little boy-bear and carried him," she went on, as though loath to leave the story. "Looking at the woman-bear I saw that she had noticed me pick up her baby, and that she was standing up. When a bear that is standing up drops down again it always travels in the direction in which its head points when its front paws touch the ground. This woman-bear came back down to the ground with her head toward us, so that we women knew she was coming after us. This gave us a good start, but I had to drop the baby just the same. Tst, tst, tst.

"We liked pets, we women, even though they made extra work for us. I once knew a woman who had a crow that could talk. He was smart, and yet one of the worst thieves I ever saw. He would steal anything to make a little trouble. When the woman first got this crow she made a rawhide dress for it. This dress fitted over the bird's wings, leaving its head and tail and feet sticking out. She carried the crow with her on her horse until it learned to stay with her. Then it used to fly over the line of travois, stopping to rest, and say things, wherever it pleased. It would ride with any of us women, but never with the men, just fly down and ride awhile, or until it wanted a change. I've forgotten what finally happened to this crow-bird."

There came a gentle rapping on the door now. "Come in," I called.

Two little girls entered, timidly, one of them having visited us before. This one, the oldest, spoke to Pretty-shield in Crow; and as usual, the old woman dug down into her pouch, handed each little beggar a silver quarter, and then with a corner of her own blanket attended to the younger one's nose. "My grandchildren," she said, proudly, as the pair went out to spend the half dollar so easily gained. "Have you grand-children, Sign-talker?"

"Yes," I answered.

"How many?" she asked, interested.

"Two boys," I told her, quite proudly.

"Tst, tst, tst! No girls! I have had much work to do for my grandchildren; and I have had bad trouble sometimes. But I have tried to keep it out of my eyes," she said, half to herself, while I put some coal on the fire.

"I had another story to tell you, but I have lost it," she smiled, when I sat down again. "Maybe my grandchildren took it away from me. No, no, here it is. I have found it again.

"This happened at The-hollow-rock near The-big-drop. The leaves on the trees were nearly grown. Several of us girls were playing at kicking the ball. In this game we choose sides. A girl places the ball upon her foot, and kicks it up, keeps doing this until she misses, and the ball falls to the ground. It is then the other side's turn to kick the ball, each girl taking her turn until all have kicked. The side that keeps the ball from falling the longest time, the greatest number of kicks, wins the game; and always the winners touch the foreheads of the losers with their hands. I was a good ball kicker, but there were girls who could beat me.

"On this day that was so beautiful, we had just finished a game when my father, who had been driving his horses to water, stopped to talk to us. 'You girls had better dig some bitter-roots,' he said. 'They are quite plentiful up that way,' he pointed.

"Soup made with bitter-roots and crushed bones is very fine. We girls all liked it, so that as soon as my father rode away about his business we began to dig bitter-roots, finding many where he had said. When at last the patch played out a girl of my own age and I went farther, looking for more bitter-roots, leaving the younger girls to peel the roots we had already dug.

"We separated, I going along the edge of smooth stone on the rim of a coulee, so that I might look down for bitter-roots growing below. I came to a juniper tree growing out of a crack in the rock, a twisted, crooked juniper that was in my way. When I took hold of one of its branches to swing myself around it on the narrow ledge I saw two baby antelope on a flat place, in the shade. Each was lying with its pretty little head on the other's neck. I stood still to watch them. Only their slim ears moved. They were sound asleep. I ran back and beckoned the other girl, who came to me. I whispered, telling her about the baby antelope, just how they were lying asleep and how we might reach them. 'Let us catch them,' I proposed. 'You go around *that* way,' I showed her, 'and I will go *this* way. You catch the top one, and I will catch the other one.'

"She agreed. We slipped upon the babies, and caught them both. 'Aaaah! Aaaah! Aaaah!' they cried; 'aaaah, aaaah!' Ah, how they cried!

"We were tying their legs together so that we might carry them to the village when, 'Whiff-whiff! Whiff-whiff!' their mother came, her hair bristling, her eyes wild. She began running around us, 'Whiff-whiff!'

"'Aaaah! Aaaaah! Aaaah!' the babies cried louder than ever. Their crying made the mother crazy. Bristled like a fighting wolf she ran at us, but stopped, stamping her hoofs, her eyes full of fear and fight.

"Suddenly, as though some medicine had told her what to do, she ran to the ledge of rock, and began to beat it with her hoofs, as though beating a drum. And then she began to sing, keeping time on the rock with her hoofs. I understood her words."

Reaching for one of my pencils, Pretty-shield stood up and with it began to drum on the table-top, her intelligent face almost fanatical. "Tap-tap—tap-tap —tap-tap—tap-tap." And then she sang:

" 'Who is going to have the smartest children?
The one that has straight ears.
Get up and run; run on.'

"She sang this song four times," she said, sitting down again, the pencil yet in her hand. "I could not stand it to hear her, a mother, sing that way. I thought of how my own heart would feel if somebody stole children that belonged to me. I untied my baby antelope. 'Go,' I told it, feeling glad to see it run to its mother.

"The other girl acted as I had, and then that mother had her family again with her. I felt better," she said, leaning forward to replace the pencil on the table. "That song has never left me," she went on. "When my grandchildren are fretful at night I sing it to them, and they always go to sleep. I had to sing it last night.

"The antelope are a strange people," she said mistily. "They are beautiful to look at, and yet they are tricky. We do not trust them. They appear and disappear; they are like shadows on the plains. Because of their great beauty young men sometimes follow the antelope and are lost forever. Even if these foolish ones find themselves and return, they are never again right in their heads. This strangeness has always belonged to the antelope, as you will see by what I am now going to tell you.

"Once, long, long ago, in late summer when choke-cherries were ripening, four Crow girls were kicking the ball. They were playing beneath chokecherry trees that were heavy with blackening cherries. At the end of their first game these four girls were surprised to see two other girls standing near them in the chokecherry shade. So softly had these girls walked that the ball-kickers had not even heard their footsteps; and the strange girls were beautiful, so beautiful that the ball-kickers wondered.

" 'It is growing late. The darkness will soon be here. Let us go now to our mothers' lodges,' said one of the ball-kicking ones, looking at the shadows on the ground beside her.

" 'Will you not come to *our* lodge for a short visit?' asked one of the beautiful strangers, softly. 'It is near by, and comfortable. Our mother will be glad to see you.'

" 'Yes, let us go with these beautiful girls, and sit with them in their mother's lodge for a while,' answered one of the ball-kickers.

"And so they went, following the two beautiful ones to their mother's lodge, which was not far away.

" 'Mother, mother, we have brought some visitors

with us,' called one of the strangers, when they reached the lodge.

"'Bring them in with you, daughters,' answered a voice that was soft and cheerful.

"Inside, the mother of the two beautiful strangers gave the ball-kickers some berries to eat. And then she talked to them a little.

"At last the ball-kickers had to go home, and said so. The two beautiful ones went with them, walking always behind. The wind was blowing in the same direction that the girls were traveling. It kept growing stronger, stirring the leaves on the trees, and the grass along the trail they were following, till one of the ball-kickers said: 'Don't you think that our new friends smell like the deer-people? The wind keeps telling me this over and over again.'

"'No,' laughed the other ball-kickers. 'We are in deer country. It is the deer-people themselves that you smell.'

"'Well, perhaps,' said the first, 'but anyhow I think there is something very queer about these new friends of ours. I feel a little afraid.'

"'Let us ask them to come into my mother's lodge,' said one of the ball-kickers, when they had reached the Crow village.

"'Good,' agreed the others. But the beautiful ones

said, 'No, there are too many boys and dogs here. We will go home now, and some time we will come again to visit you.'

" 'If you will not forget to do this we will walk part way back with you,' offered the ball-kickers. And they *did* walk back, the strange beautiful ones again walking behind, until one of the ball-kickers said, 'I can see your mother's lodge from here. We shall have to turn back.'

" 'Oh, we can go on alone from here,' laughed the strange beautiful ones, waiting for the ball-kickers to turn back.

"But the ball-kicking Crow girls, instead of turning back, only stepped aside, so that the strange beautiful ones might pass. Ahhh! Now, for the first time, the ball-kickers saw the hind-ends of their new friends. They were *antelope!*

"The Crow girls, glad to be rid of the strange beautiful ones, spat four times on the ground, over their left hands. Ahhh, the antelope are deceivers, not helpers."

The antelope, beautiful, and strangely marked is so camouflaged by nature that one has difficulty in seeing them on their native plains until they present their rumps in flight.

NINE

"D<small>ID</small> any of the animal-people ever talk to you, Sign-talker?" Pretty-shield asked, abruptly, moving her chair forward, her manner confidential.

When I told her that I had often understood what my horse or my dog wished me to know, she did not appear to be satisfied. As though pondering, she stared at the blank wall over my head, disappointment in her eyes. "But they *do* talk," she said, firmly, half to herself. Then, "You have asked me for only a woman's story, and I have found one. It is about a woman I

used to know, a woman and a mouse; and even the mouse was a woman-mouse, so I will tell you the story.

"Once in the summertime we moved our lodges from the Bighorn mountains to the plains, so that we might follow the buffalo herds. Our men had been hunting deer and bighorns in the mountains for a whole moon. We were glad to get back to the plains. There were not many lodges of us, about sixty, and of course we had lost track of our enemies while we had been in the mountains, so that when we camped again on the plains everybody was watchful; and everybody was hungry for buffalo meat. The men went out to run buffalo even before our lodges were up.

"One of these men, named Muskrat-that-shows, asked his woman for something to eat before he left the camp. The woman, Little-face, opened a pouch to get him some pemmican, and saw a woman-mouse, and her children, in the pouch. She did not disturb them, but opened another pouch, gave her man some pemmican, and then, being tired after the long move, laid down on her robe to rest. She had no children. Nothing disturbed her, and she slept.

" 'My friend! My friend!' Somebody was whispering in her ear. 'In four days your people will be attacked by the Lacota. Can you make the men believe this, get them to go back to the place that you came from? The Lacota war-party numbers many more than the men in these sixty lodges. I am worried about my children.'

"The woman, sitting up now, saw the woman-mouse on her robe. 'Get up. Go out, and do something quickly,' urged the woman-mouse, sitting up straight.

"The woman did get up, did go out, and did tell her mother what she had dreamed, what the woman-mouse had said to her. Then she began at once to pack up her things.

"A wolf, named Red-bear, who was head man of

our sixty lodges, was watching the country from a hill near our camp. The woman's mother called to him, made signs to come in.

"Red-bear knew that the woman would not call unless something was wrong in the camp. He came, listened to what the woman and her daughter had to say, and then acted quickly. 'I, too, have felt that some trouble was near us,' he said, riding out on the plains to find the hunters.

"The hunters had already killed several buffalo, and were gathered round a cow that had a Cheyenne arrow sticking in her side. Red-bear and the others knew at once that the arrow had not been long out of its quiver, so that when Red-bear told what the woman-mouse had told Little-face, the woman of Muskrat-that-shows, everybody was ready to get away from that country, even though there were many buffalo handy.

"Muskrat-that-shows had followed a herd of buffalo, and was nowhere in sight. One man went to find him, and the rest returned to the camp with only the tongues of the buffalo they had killed. Down came all the sixty lodges that had so lately been set up, and in came the horses. The women were packing the travois, the children running about, when suddenly Muskrat-that-shows, and the man who had gone to look for him, came in with news. He said that he had seen three people on the plains, that they were so far away he could not at first tell if they were people or wolves. He set up some little sticks of sage to see if the black specks were moving, Yes, they were moving, and they were people, one of them very small. He said he believed them to be women."

Whenever an object on the plains was so distant that the unaided eye could not determine if it moved, Indians, and even white plainsmen, set up two sticks, stalks of grass, or sage. By sighting over these two points, in line with the suspicious object, its slightest movement was made discernible.

"I noticed that the buffalo on the plains were moving now, as though hunters were after them," Pretty-shield went on. "I wanted to get away from that place, feeling glad when we started. I feared that Red-bear and Muskrat-that-shows, who had gone back to look for the people who might be women, would be killed. The afternoon was hot, so hot that our horses were lazy, and yet we made them travel fast. Red-bear had told us where we must stop for the night without pitching our lodges. 'In the morning you must go on, even though you do not see Muskrat-that-shows and me,' he said. By the time we got started the buffalo on the plains were moving faster. I felt very much afraid that we should never get away without a fight.

"We reached the place where we had been told to stop without seeing the enemy, and just before dark. Unpacking the horses and travois, we ate something and lay down without pitching a single lodge. There were men with our horses, and wolves on the hills, and yet I felt afraid. The night was cool. A nice wind had come and there were many stars in the sky. I slept.

"Late in the night a dog growled near me. I sat up; then everybody sat up. Red-bear and Muskrat-that-shows had come in with two Crow women and a little girl, who had been slaves to the Lacota. The little girl was crying. I got up and went to help her. Her buckskin dress was in shreds. Her lips were cracked and swollen by the sun, her moccasins gone, and her feet cracked open and very sore. She was about my own age, about nine or ten snows. My mother rubbed hot fat on the girl's lips and feet. Ah, I pitied that little girl. Her name was One-woman. She lately died here, an old woman, like myself."

Pretty-shield's fist went to her forehead. "Her mother's name was Lion-woman," she said, after a minute. "How they suffered, these three, on the long journey out of the Lacota country. They lived on grasshoppers. Lion-woman, the little girl's mother, was the prettiest woman I ever saw," she said, brightening.

"When we reached the Bighorn river we saw the Crow village on the other side, and our hearts sang. The little girl, riding double with me, laughed and cried at the same time. But the water was yet high, so that we were slow getting across to where the village stood.

"The news of finding the women was already in the Crow village. Our people were careful. Our wolves were always out, and a wolf from the village had met us and then carried the story over the Bighorn long before we reached it. I shall never forget how the little girl's father hugged her, nor that he cut off one of his fingers to show his grief for the suffering the Lacota had caused his woman and his daughter. They had been gone two whole snows. He had thought them dead, and had taken another woman. But now that Lion-woman had returned he took her to his lodge as though she had not been away. She had children even after this."

"And is this all of the story?" I asked, because Pretty-shield seemed to have finished.

"No," she said. "The woman, Little-face, who found the woman-mouse in the pouch, carried her all summer in a rawhide bag. She fed the mouse and her children, letting them all play about as they wished when night came and the lodge was pitched. But the young ones did not stay long. They all ran away to find places for themselves. The woman-mouse asked to be taken back to the mountains when the winter was coming on. She did not like the plains. She wished to be where there were pine trees, so one day Little-face carried the woman-mouse into the mountains, found a nice hole beneath a big pine tree, and let her friend go into it. 'I will always hear you if you call me,' said the woman-mouse, looking up at Little-face.

"After this Little-face would never step on a little hole in the ground, never. She always walked around little holes that were in the ground, because she feared that she might disturb the mice-people. They were her medicine, and helped her. Even Red-bear often asked advice from this woman. I have now finished this story."

"What about the owl? Do you like him?" I asked.

"No, not the great owl," she answered. "We *do* like the long-legged prairie owl that lives with the prairie-dogs. An arrow always misses the long-legged owl. He is big medicine. My father's medicine was the long-legged owl that lives with the prairie-dogs."

She bent her head, pressing her clenched fist against her forehead. "Before I came on this world, and even for a time afterward, my people saw strange things, heard words spoken that they did not always understand," she said, so softly that Goes-together leaned to listen. "Now they see nothing, hear nothing that is strange," she went on, a little louder. And then, as though she had decided some question within herself, she moved her chair nearer the table, and looked into my eyes. "I once had a vision, Sign-talker, but you had better not write it down," she advised.

"It came to me soon after I got this scar on my forehead. I was about eight years old. The moon was the one that ripens the berries, and our village, a large one with more lodges than I could count, was at the mouth of Deer creek. There is a place there where the water whips the bank, as though angry. Beneath the water just there, one may see a black hole, with the white water sucking into it. We call this place The-alligator's-lodge. If one were to be sucked into this black hole he would never come out again; no, never."

Crow story tellers, although a plains people, frequently mention the alligator, and even sea-monsters, leading me to believe that the tribe at one time lived in the South, by the sea.

"On this day, just when I wanted badly to go with

some young women to pick berries, an old woman who had nobody to help her, asked me to bring her a kettle of water. Taking her kettle I ran to Deer creek that was but a little way from the lodges, hoping yet to catch up with the young women who had already started for the berry patches.

"When I reached the creek, that was not far from the lodges, I saw three naked women sitting on the bank above The-alligator's-lodge, that black hole that sucks in the white water. They were young, and had unbraided their hair, so that it hung loosely about their shoulders. They were strangers to me. I wondered if they knew that the black hole was there. I called out to warn them.

"Instantly the three women slid down the bank, like turtles, into the white water, and were sucked into The-alligator's-lodge. They were gone! It was as though they had never been on the bank at all.

"Frightened now, I bent to dip the old woman's kettle into the water at the place where we always got our water from Deer creek. But I did not dip it. The water that had always been deep there was now shallow. And"—here Pretty-shield stood up, her hand on the table—"on the bottom, on the little stones, I saw a woman looking up at me. She was not a Crow woman, not like any woman that I had ever seen. She was a *Person* [sprite]. Her hair was yellow, her eyes blue, and her ears were long and notched.

"I screamed; but remember nothing more, except that when I again wakened I was in my mother's lodge, with my face painted red [death paint]. I have never been near The-alligator's-lodge since that day," she finished, sitting down.

"Ahhh, you have written down my words," she said, reproachfully. "If you put them into a book nobody who can read will believe them; and yet they tell only the truth.

"There are times in our lives when we see strange things, hear words that we do not understand," she went on cryptically. "When my sister died I went into the mountains to mourn for her. After fasting for four days and nights I walked the high hills and ridges until my feet were sore. There was snow on the ridges, even snow on the plains, and all about me I saw the tracks of some animal I did not know. They were everywhere; and yet I gave them little notice until I heard, 'Ho-ho—ho-ho,' a little way ahead of me. Looking, I saw two black animals, not much larger than prairie-dogs, go into two holes in the rock. To this day I do not know what those animals were; and yet they helped me, because I let them.

"Ahh, how women used to mourn! Their blood-

covered faces come to me yet. They sadden me, sometimes. How often, when I was a little girl, I covered
my head with a robe and cried when I heard them
wailing alone on the hills. I knew, even then, that
some day I should mourn, and that like them I should
feel myself to be alone on the world."

TEN

"TELL me of your marriage, about your man," I suggested.

Her face lighted. "Ahhh, I was sixteen when my man, Goes-ahead, took me. I have already told you that my father had promised me to Goes-ahead, when I was thirteen. When I became sixteen years old my father kept his promise."

"Did you fall in love with him before he took you?" I asked.

"No, no," she smiled. "I had not often spoken to him until he took me. Then I fell in love with him, because he loved me and was always kind. Young women did not then fall in love, and get married to please themselves, as they now do. They listened to their fathers, married the men selected for them, and this, I believe, is the best way. There were no deformed children born in those days," she said, thoughtfully. "And men and women were happier, too, I feel sure," she added, with a challenge in her words. "A man could not take a woman from his own clan, no matter how much he might wish to have her.

He had to marry a woman belonging to another clan, and then all their children belonged to their mother's clan. This law kept our blood strong."

"Did your man, Goes-ahead, have another woman when he took you?" I asked, knowing their custom.

"Yes, my oldest sister, Standing-medicine-rock, was his first woman; then he took me, and finally, when my youngest sister, Two-scalps, became sixteen years old, she was also taken by my man, Goes-ahead, so that there were three lodges, all sisters, and all belonging to Goes-ahead.

"But I was the only one who gave him children," she added, eagerly. "It was *my* face that he painted when he had gained that right by saving a Crow warrior's life in battle. And it was I who rode his warhorse and carried his shield. Ahh, I felt proud when my man painted my face," she said, softly, her eyes lighted by her thoughts. "After this I had the right to paint my face whenever there was a big feast or a big dance; and I did it because it was only showing respect for my man, Goes-ahead."

"Did you always get along well together, you three sisters, who were wives of Goes-ahead?" I asked.

"I will hide nothing from you, Sign-talker. Standing-medicine-rock, my oldest sister, was not a very good woman. I mean that she liked other men, and that she sometimes forgot she belonged to Goes-ahead. I knew about this, and talked to her. But I did not tell on her. It was my brother's duty to do this, according to our tribal custom, and not mine, so that I only talked to her. But my talking did no good. And yet Standing-medicine-rock, my oldest sister, was a good worker. There was nothing lazy about her. There were few women who could dress a robe better than she could, none who kept a neater lodge, and not many who looked nicer; and yet she was not a very good woman. My youngest sister, Two-scalps, was different. We got along well together. I helped her all I could, and she helped me; and we both helped our mother, who was growing old.

"My father was already an old man. He needed a young hunter to help him kill meat, so that I felt happy with my man, Goes-ahead, who was always a lucky hunter. Our lodges all had plenty of fat meat, even my father's, because my man, Goes-ahead, was generous when my father grew old.

"And now when the young will not listen, when my own grandchildren pay no attention to what I tell them I think of my man, Goes-ahead, and do my best to save. I am willing to go without food, to be hungry, that they may have plenty to eat, and yet, now-a-days, this is not enough. There are too many new things, too few who follow old customs. I, myself, get lost when I look and listen, and my grandchildren are all eyes and ears. Looking and listening to these new things, many of them bad, my grandchildren are like the dry earth when rain falls upon it."

"Tell me about your man, Goes-ahead," I said, to turn her thoughts away from her grandchildren.

"I like to think of him," she said, brightening. "I will talk to you about him, even though we Crows do not often speak of the dead. I am willing to tell you anything I know."

"Was he a large man?" I asked, because she did not go on.

"No. He was a small man. And he was brave, and kindly. He never counted coup in battle," she said, a little regretfully, I thought, "and yet the council gave him the right to paint my face, because he saved a Crow's life in a fight with the Nez Percé."

"Could a woman's uncle, who had counted coup, paint her face if her own man did not possess this right?" I asked, wishing to lead her to talk of tribal customs.

"Yes," she said. "If a man who had not counted coup married after reaching the age of twenty-five, as he had a right to do, his woman might get her uncle to paint her face, if the uncle had counted coup in battle. But her man had first to ask permission to have his woman's face painted by her uncle, so that everybody knew about it. Not many women liked to have their faces painted by anybody besides their own men, because it made talk. Besides it was like a borrowed thing."

Then as though she had guessed why I had asked the question, she went on. "When I was young a woman whose man had never stolen an enemy's horse was not permitted to ride a horse at any tribal ceremony. I have seen women pulled from horses by the men because they had forgotten this law."

"Tell me more about your life in the villages."

"War, killing meat, and bringing it into camp, horse-stealing, and taking care of horses, gave our men plenty of hard work; and they had to be in shape to fight at any time, day or night. We women had our children to care for, meat to cook, and to dry, robes to dress, skins to tan, clothes, lodges, and moccasins to make. Besides these things we not only pitched the lodges, but took them down and packed the horses and the travois, when we moved camp; yes, and we gathered the wood for our fires, too. We were busy, especially when we were going to move. I loved to move, even after I was a married woman with children to take care of. Moving made me happy."

"Tell me how you made pemmican, how you made paint hold its color, about your work as a married woman," I suggested.

"Pemmican! Ahh, when I think of pemmican I grow hungry," she smiled, good-naturedly. "We cut good, lean meat into strips and dried it a little; then roasted it until it looked brown. After this was done we pounded the dry meat with stone hammers that are found nearly everywhere. They were made by The-ones-who-lived-without-fire. Next we soaked ripe chokeberries in water, and then used this water to boil crushed bones. When the kettle of boiled bones was cool we skimmed off the grease from the bone-marrow, mixed it with the pounded meat, poured this into buffalo heart-skins, and let it get solid. When it was taken out to eat— Ah, I have made myself hungry. Where is the sun, Sign-talker?" she asked, looking at the window.

"Eleven," I signed, looking at my watch.

"I must not forget my grandchildren; but there is yet time to talk a little. Paint," she went on, remembering my questions, "we made hold its color with the gum, the water-colored gum, that one sees on the chokecherry trees; and we used buffalo-hoofs, too. We boiled them until they trembled [jellied], mixed this with our paint, let it dry, and then cut it into squares. Water or grease made the color come again from these squares, any time, after this was done."

"And the *ah-stah-dah*, the skin-lodges; how many buffalo skins did a lodge require, and how many poles?" I asked because she did not go on.

"From twelve to twenty skins, and from fourteen to twenty-four poles, according to the size of the lodge. We Crows had big lodges and little lodges, just as white men have big houses and small ones."

"And how did you tan your robes and skins? What did you use?"

"The liver and brains of the animals, and sometimes the cotton from the cottonwoods was added, when it was handy. We dressed many robes to trade for things we wanted."

"Where was the woman's place in the lodge?" I asked.

"On either side of the door," she said, arranging her blanket.

"What roots did you dig?" I persisted.

"Turnips, carrots, stinking-turnips, bitter-roots, and potatoes. They are nearly always plentiful in the Crow country. And besides, there was the bear's food. I will go now, Sign-talker. My mind is sleepy."

"This summer I am going to make myself a good

tepee, Sign-talker," Pretty-shield said upon her return. "I am tired of living in my place. A good tepee is nicer."

"Are you a lodge-cutter?" I asked, knowing that not many Crow women are called "lodge-cutters."

"Yes," she replied; "and so was my mother. Did you ever know of a woman having a painted lodge, Sign-talker?" she asked.

"No," I said.

"Well, I once knew a woman who had a painted lodge. Her name was Good-otter. My mother cut the lodge for her, and a Lacota slave-man, who had lived with us nearly all his life, painted it. This slave's name was Tricky-wolf. I have never seen a prettier lodge than Good-otter's. It fitted its poles like a leaf-tepee, and was well painted. On each side of the skewers there was a red strip reaching all the way to the ground. On its back was a mountain lion, and an otter breathing red fire from its open mouth. I believe that some of Good-otter's relatives may yet have that painted lodge, because it was big medicine, even though it was a woman's lodge."

Women did not paint lodges, and only wise-ones (medicine-men) possessed them, the characters that had appeared in their medicine-dreams being depicted on their lodge-skins. Few women were "lodge-cutters," the right to cut them being distinctive, a mark of both character and ability. Sewing the lodge-skins was done by all women. They feasted and visited as they worked, much as our mothers did at "quilting bees." Little girls at play frequently made lodges of leaves, often of a single leaf, that were marvels of form, so that whenever a newly made lodge-skin covered its poles perfectly it was said to "fit like a leaf-tepee."

"Where was a visitor's place in a lodge?" I asked.

"On either side of the head [center, at back], where the man of the lodge sat," she answered. "And when a man wished to visit another man in his lodge he stopped by the door and called out, 'Are you there?' If the friend wanted company he asked the visitor to come in and set fat meat before him, and they smoked and talked together. A woman wishing to visit always lifted up the lodge-door and peeped inside. But unless asked to come in all visitors went about their own business, without getting mad over not being invited into lodges.

"When old people were the visitors they were given dried tenderloin from which all sinew had been stripped. This fine meat was first dried, and then pounded up and mixed with bone-marrow. It was served to old men in bowls made of box-elder wood, about so large [about six inches in diameter]. Old women got theirs on squares of rawhide. We pounded our meat on stones held together with rawhide, using the long stones that were made by Those-who-lived-without-fire [stone pestles]. I wonder what my grandmother would have thought about having to eat white men's cows," she mused, wonderingly; adding, "Their meat smells so different."

"Did you have regular meals, regular times to eat?" I asked.

This pleased her. "Not as white people do," she laughed. "We ate in the morning before the hunters went out, and again in the evening after they had returned, and any other time when we were hungry. And yet," she added, quite seriously, "I can remember but four fat women in all the Crow tribe of those days. I can name them. They were Alkali, Otter-that-comes-up, Fire, and Young-turtle. They were all fat women, and yet they were lively enough for anybody. They had to be lively to get along in those days."

"You have told me how you made pemmican. Tell me how you dried meat," I said.

"We first cut up the meat, taking it off the animal in the sections that naturally divide it. Then we split these sections, and spread the meat on racks in the sun, turning it often. At night we took the meat off the racks, piled it on the ground, covered the pile with a buffalo robe, and then trampled upon it to squeeze out all the blood that might yet be in the meat. When morning came again we respread the meat in the sunshine, being careful not to let the meat touch the racks in the same places as before. If a woman were careless about this she might lose her meat, because the spots that had touched the racks would spoil unless changed every day until the meat was dry. I wish I had some of that good buffalo meat right now to take to my place," she said, getting up to move her chair away from the stove.

"Did you ever make fire with flint and steel?" I asked.

"Oh, yes, many times; and before the horse came our people made fire with two hard stones, and even with sticks. I have heard my grandmother tell of this, but never tried it myself. Last summer," she said, leaning toward me, confidentially, "two old men had a race to see which could first start a fire with two hard stones. I was standing very near the old man who won this fire-race, and saw that he held the head of a match so that the stones would strike it, and make a fire," she confided, her eyes twinkling. "I didn't tell on him," she added hastily. "No, I kept still, because the old man showed smartness."

"Did you women often butcher buffalo on the plains and bring them into camp?" I asked.

"No. The men killed the meat, butchered it, and packed it into camp, unless there was some special reason for the women having to do it. I will tell you what happened to a friend of mine when she was butchering a buffalo on the plains.

"A small band of us had camped on the ground now covered by the white man's city of Terry. We were afraid of attack by the Lacota, and because there were but few warriors with us most of them were kept in camp. Two men went out to kill buffalo. To save time, one of them took his woman along to do the butchering. This man, knowing that if he had to leave his woman to butcher one buffalo while he killed another the Lacota might come upon her, gave her his fastest horse to ride.

"When a buffalo is struck with arrows it sometimes runs far before it falls. On this day the first buffalo fell down a long way out on the plains from our camp. The woman stopped beside it, tying her horse to the dead buffalo's horns, and began at once to butcher it. Her man had told her that if the Lacota came she must not try to untie the rope that held her horse, but that she must cut it with her knife, and ride fast. Buffalo were all around her; and just where the dead one was lying there were many deeply worn trails that herds of buffalo had made. One of these trails, the one nearest to the dead buffalo, had been washed out by the waters of melting snows, so that it was deeper than any of the others.

"The woman, working rapidly, was bending over the dead buffalo, when she heard her horse snort and move, pulling on his rope. Turning her head she saw a bull, a mad one, coming on the run.

"She sprang toward her horse; but he shied! She missed him! Ho! The bull was upon her. She ran around the dead buffalo; and so did the horse, with the mad bull after them both. Three times she jumped across the deeply cut trail, with the frightened horse ahead of her, and the mad bull behind. When she came to it the fourth time she threw herself into it, face downward.

"The mad bull did not miss her," said Pretty-shield, breathing heavily. "He kept after the horse that could not get away. Round and round he went, with the mad bull after him, both jumping the deep trail where the woman was lying; right over her back each time, until the horse's rope was so tightly wound around the dead buffalo that the horse had to stop.

"The mad bull ripped him to pieces, tossing his hot flesh and blood upon the woman's back. Then he tore the dead buffalo to bits. When his fierce snorting stopped the deep trail was filled with pieces of both the horse and the buffalo. The woman's clothes were soaked with blood, and yet she waited a long time before she lifted her head to look around. When she did look she saw the mad bull walking slowly away, as though he had worn himself out. She waited until he disappeared over a hill, and then got up and ran. The man said that the place where this happened was bad to look at," she finished, tired by her recital.

"There were queer buffalo, just as there are queer people," she went on, after a minute. "Once, after I was married and had a baby, my brother, Other-gun, brought me a buffalo calf, and this calf was a queer one. I saddled it and put my little baby girl, Pine-fire, on its back, leading the calf about the village with the laughing child riding it. My brother objected to this. 'If you intend to eat that calf you'd better not play with it,' he told me. And my father said, 'Let it go back to the herd.' But I wished to keep the calf, because Pine-fire looked so pretty on its back.

"That evening when my father asked me if I had let the calf go free I was going to tell him that I had, when the little buffalo trotted up to me as though he wanted to stay. He saved me from telling a lie. But my father did not like to have the calf in the village.

143

He said that he was afraid something might happen to my own child if I kept the calf from its mother. 'Either kill it and eat it, or let it go free,' he said. And then he took the calf back to the herd.

"The next morning the calf was standing by my lodge-door when I wakened. He had come back in the night. 'There is something strange about this,' my man, Goes-ahead, said, going after my father. And then my man and my father took the calf again to the herd, and let it go. My father said that this time, when he set it free, the calf kicked up its heels, rolled, as though glad to be back with his people, and that when it went away with the herd it seemed to him to have grown up, to be as large as any of the others. There was something queer about that calf."

She turned here to talk to Goes-together, taking the latter's sewing in her hands for inspection. The merry mood that I had particularly noticed upon her arrival at the school building had departed, and now she appeared to have lost interest in her story telling.

ELEVEN

"Will you tell me about the care of newly born babies, just what was done to make them comfortable; and all about it?" I asked.

"Yes, Sign-talker," she answered, readily. "We Crow women had no trouble when our babies were born. I will tell you everything about it. I will do this by relating my own first experience. I have had five children, three girls and two boys. I lost a boy and a girl when they were babies. Now all my girls are gone. But my boy, Good, is living, and I have never known him to be bad. He lives up to the name I gave him. I will tell you about my daughters, Pine-fire and Little-woman, when you ask me.

"Now I am going to begin at the beginning, because everything was so different when I was young. I was expecting a baby, of course, but was not worrying about it. One day while playing with some girl friends I felt a little, quick pain, and sat down, laughing about it. One of my friends guessed what was about to happen, and told my mother.

"But when my mother, and a wise-one, named Left-hand, came after me I did not wish to go to the lodge with them. 'Yes,' my mother urged, 'come. We have pitched a new lodge for you, daughter.'

"Left-hand's lodge was pitched near my mother's. I noticed now that one of my father's best horses, with several fine robes on his back, was tied there. My father had already paid her for helping me, even before I needed help. Old Left-hand wore a buffalo robe with the hair-side out. Her face was painted with mud, her hair was tied in a big lump on her forehead, and in her hand she carried some of the-grass-that-the-buffalo-do-not-eat. Her eyes were so full of fun that I laughed at her as I might have laughed at a mud-clown. And yet she was serious, even solemn in all her actions.

"Now I must tell you about the lodge they had pitched for me. Left-hand stopped me just inside the door. A fire was burning, and my mother had made my bed, a soft buffalo robe folded with the hair side out. This bed was not to lie down on. Crow women do not lie down when their babies are born, nor even afterward, excepting to sleep when night comes, as others do. Two stakes had been driven into the ground for me to take hold of, and robes had been rolled up and piled against them, so that when I knelt on the bed-robe and took hold of the two stakes, my elbows would rest upon the pile of rolled robes.

"While I stood by the door, Left-hand took four live coals from the lodge-fire. One of these she placed on the ground at the door, then one to the left, halfway to the head [center of back], one at the head, and one in front of the bed-robe, which was on the right of the door, halfway between it and the head of the lodge. Then she dropped a little of the-grass-that-the-buffalo-do-not-eat upon each of these coals, telling me to walk to the left, to go around to my bed [as the sun goes], stepping over the coals.

" 'Walk as though you are busy,' she said, brushing my back with the tail of her buffalo robe, and grunting as a buffalo-cow grunts.

"I had stepped over the second coal when I saw that I should have to *run* if I reached my bed-robe in time. I *jumped* the third coal, and the *fourth,* knelt down on the robe, took hold of the two stakes; and my first child, Pine-fire, was there with us.

"It was always like this, in the old days. There must be some reason for the change. I have wondered about it. Perhaps it is because women have grown proud. Yes, I believe that this must be the reason," she finished, as simply as she had begun.

In her description of the maternity lodge Pretty-shield placed a common kitchen chair, with its hard seat toward her, its back representing the two stakes, its seat the pile of rolled robes, and knelt to show me the exact position she had assumed at the birth of her daughter.

As though compelled by its proffered comparison of two eras I glanced at a picture on the schoolroom wall above her head. There was a beautiful, blue-eyed, fair-haired baby lying upon a snow-white bed; and this ominous warning: "Protect him against diphtheria *now*. Your doctor can do it with toxin antitoxin."

"And what happened next?" I asked.

"I stood up, when it was time," she said, simply, "and then old Left-hand wound a strip of tanned buffalo skin around my waist. After this she greased my baby with grease that had red paint mixed with it, dusting a little powdered buffalo-chips and finely pounded clay from its hips down to its knees. Next she put a layer of the hair from a buffalo's head all around the child, and wrapped her in soft buckskin before laying her on a strip of stiff buffalo rawhide to keep her little head from falling backward. After this was all done Left-hand wrapped my baby in tanned calf-skin, and handed her to me. Her work was done, so that she could go about her own business.

"Each night all this dressing was removed, the baby washed, and again greased, and then left to kick up its heels on a soft buffalo robe until the new wrappings were ready for it. At first we never washed new-born babies. A little later on when they could stand it without danger we washed them every night, the boys in cold water, and the girls in warm water, when we had it. Boy-babies are always tougher than girls."

"When did you put babies into back-cradles?"

"When they were six moons old," she replied. "Until that time we carried babies in our arms, even on horseback. After they were put into back-cradles they were much less trouble. But when they grew old enough to ride on top of packs and on travois, they began again to require watching. At four snows of age a Crow child could take good care of itself, on foot, or on a gentle horse."

"But you women did not work for a time after a baby was born to you, did you?" I asked.

"Oh, yes," she smiled. "But we took short steps when we walked, and ate nothing and drank nothing that was warm, for a whole moon. Besides this, when the village moved and we had to ride, we tied our legs together just above our knees, sitting on flat packs with our babies in our arms, and our feet sticking out in front of us—one foot on each side of the horse's neck. We had to be helped on and off a horse of course, with our legs tied together, but this did not last longer than one moon."

TWELVE

Pretty-shield's words, "My mind is sleepy," warned me that she might at any moment now wish to drop her story telling, and there were yet many questions I wished to ask her. I must somehow rekindle her interest. Leaving the school building I saw that the "prisoners" were raking up the leaves, as though by some secret means Pretty-shield's idea had been transmitted to those in authority. These workers, with long rakes, appeared to be a little

ashamed of their occupation, and did not lift their
eyes as I passed.

An hour later white clouds were scudding; and a
sharp wind that came from the wide plains was scat-
tering the damp leaves that had been raked into piles.
"More work for the wicked," I thought, walking on
toward the school building. And then four chickadees
landed in a bush beside the walk, their busy little
bodies giving me an idea. Every tribe of Indians in
the Northwest respects the chickadee. They possess
many stories about him and greatly enjoy telling them

to friends. I would try to get Pretty-shield going again by introducing the chickadee.

But I could not make our interpreter, Goes-together, understand which bird I meant. To her, as to most moderns, red or white, a bird is a bird. To these unfortunates there are "little" birds and "big" birds, and here their ornithology ends. I did not know the sign for chickadee, and during all the talking between Goes-together and myself Pretty-shield's face remained amusedly blank. At last, in desperation, I whistled the spring-call of the chickadee, and the day was saved. Pretty-shield reacted instantly. She stood up and with a hand resting on the table, leaned toward me, her eyes shining.

"Ahhh, Ahh! The chickadee is big medicine, Sign-talker," she said, with one hand. "Do you know him well?" she asked so eagerly that I felt my assurance slipping.

But, "Yes," I answered, yet believing in my knowledge of the bird. I had written many stories about him.

"Good!" she signed, emphatically. "Then you have seen his tongue."

Now what was this? Was she joking? No. I knew that she was serious, and that here, as in so many other instances where old Indians had taught me, I should learn a new lesson. "No. I have not looked at the chickadee's tongue," I admitted, feeling like a trifling school-boy.

"Ahhhh!" Pretty-shield sank back into her chair, her face so fallen that I laughed outright. "Tst, tst, tst," she clucked, seemingly unable to believe that I, who could whistle the chickadee's call, did not know about the bird's tongue.

But I intended now to learn. "Tell me about his tongue, Pretty-shield," I begged, again whistling his spring-call to salve her disgust for my ignorance.

"In the fall, when the leaves first begin to change their color," she began, "the chickadee has but *one* tongue. In the springtime, when he begins to say those words you have just spoken [his spring-call] he has *seven* tongues," she said, moving her chair up to the table to place her hand flat upon its top, palm downward.

"It is by the chickadee's tongue that we tell what moon of the winter we are in," she went on, speaking rapidly. "In the first moon the chickadee shows *two* tongues, then *three,* then *four,* then *five,* then *six,* and finally *seven,*" she declared, the index finger of her right hand marking imaginary divisions upon the left, that was yet lying flat upon the table-top. "And then," she smiled, "the chickadee says 'summer's near, summer's near,' and goes back to *one* tongue."

She leaned back now. "We do not harm the chicka-dee when we look at his tongue to see what moon of the winter we are in," she assured me. "We catch them, look quickly at their tongues, and then let them go again."

I could not help feeling doubt in all this. And yet I was determined to investigate; and I did. For days, even weeks, the chickadees, usually plentiful here at Goose Bay, avoided the place as though their "medi-cine" had warned them of me. It was in April, a little too late in the season to find seven well-defined tongues, as Pretty-shield had said, when I caught two chickadees. With the aid of a jeweler's glass I dis-covered that their tongues were not alike, one having four sharp points resembling the spines on the cactus plant, two on the right, and two on the left of the tongue's center; the other, seven thread-like strands resembling a raveled edge of cloth. I thought that both tongues were shorter than the beaks seemed to warrant, there being room in each beak for a longer tongue than was present. Anyhow, the tongue of the chickadee is phenomenal and a careful examination of it late in February or early in March may prove Pretty-shield's contention to be correct.

"One day in the moon when leaves are on the ground [November] I was walking with my grand-

mother near some bushes that were full of chickadees," Pretty-shield continued. "They had been stealing fat from meat that was on the racks in the village,
and because they were full they were all laughing. I
thought it would be fun to see them all fly, and tossed
a dry buffalo-chip into the bushes. I was a very little
girl, too little to know any better, and yet my grandmother told me that I had done wrong. She took me
into her arms, and walking to another bush, where
the frightened chickadees had stopped, she said: 'This
little girl is my granddaughter. She will never again
throw anything at you. Forgive her, little ones. She
did not know any better.' Then she sat down with me
in her lap, and told me that long before this she had
lost a close friend because the woman had turned the
chickadees against her."

Here Pretty-shield was interrupted. A Crow
woman, wearing a green blanket, came to tell her that
a young man who had been missing for several days
had been found dead, and buried in a shallow grave.
His head had been split with an axe, she said.

"Bad!" Pretty-shield signed to me, when the woman
had gone. "The young man was a little crazy." Then,
as though there was nothing that she could do to help
matters, Pretty-shield took up her story telling.

"My grandmother's name was Seven-stars," she

said. "She was a wise-one. She would have only black horses; and her medicine was the chickadee. She told me that one day when her first child, a little girl, was just beginning to walk, she was dressing a buffalo robe. She said that the day was beautiful, and the moon the last one of winter.

"She and another woman, whose name was Buffalo-that-walks, had built a fire among some bushes, and both were working on robes that were pegged to the ground, with the fire burning between them. My grandmother's little girl, who became my mother, was walking and falling down, and getting up only to fall down again, all around the fire while the women worked on their robes.

"A chickadee flew into a bush beside Buffalo-that-walks. 'Summer's near, summer's near,' he said, over and over, while he hopped about in the bush.

"Buffalo-that-walks was a cross woman. 'Be quiet,' she said to the little chickadee. 'Don't you believe that I have eyes? I can see that the summer is near as well as you can. Go away. You are bothering me.'

" 'Summer's near, summer's near,' called the bird, paying no attention to what she said. 'Summer's near, summer's near.'

"Buffalo-that-walks threw a stick at the chickadee, and he dodged it. 'Ho!' he laughed, hopping higher.

'Yes, I suppose I do bother you,' he said, looking down at her with his black head turned sidewise. 'I bother nearly everybody. And now I will bother you a little more. You are going to be wrapped up in that very robe that you are making so soft. I came here to tell you this, and you threw a stick at me.'

"Then the chickadee flew to a bush that was near my grandmother. 'Summer's near, summer's near,' he said, as though there was nothing else he could think about. My grandmother picked up her little girl. The chickadee had made her afraid. 'I threw no sticks at you,' she said, starting toward her lodge with her child in her arms.

" 'Wait! Do not leave your work. Pay no attention to what the Chickadee-person has said. He will say anything that comes to his mind. Nobody believes his words,' called Buffalo-that-walks.

"My grandmother turned to look back at the woman, her friend. 'Don't say such things,' she warned. 'And I wish you would leave me out of all this foolishness. I am afraid.' Then she went on to her lodge with her little girl. Later she brought some fine back-fat to the bushes, putting it where she thought the chickadee would find it. And he did find it.

"He came while yet my grandmother was there. 'Don't worry,' he told her, picking at the back-fat.

'You are not in this trouble. You have nothing to worry about. It's the other one.'

"Buffalo-that-walks died that very night, and they wrapped her in that very robe, as the chickadee had said. Grandmother told me that as soon as Buffalo-that-walks was put away the village moved, and that the dead woman's man did not go with the village. He stayed behind to mourn for his woman.

"While he was sitting by the tree that held his woman's body the chickadee came to him. The man smoked deer-tobacco, offering his pipe to the chickadee. 'I am sorry that my woman mistreated you,' he said. 'I wish you would be my friend, chickadee.' The little bird sat on the man's hand, and talked to him. 'I am small,' he said. 'My strength is not great. I only run errands for the big ones, and yet I can help you. In the morning a *Person* will come to you. Listen to what he has to say. I must go about my own business now.'

"At daybreak, that was clear and cold and beautiful, a large bird came to the man; and the chickadee was with him. This large bird was Big-claws-on-both-sides [I could not identify this bird from her description]. He said, 'Nobody who has a good heart ever mistreats my friend, the Chickadee. Because you are sorry for what your woman did I will be your Helper for the rest of your life.' And he was a good Helper, my grandmother said.

"It was the next spring after this," Pretty-shield continued, "that one day, when my grandmother was dressing a robe, a chickadee came to her. At first it did not talk, but picked up bits of the fat in the fleshings lying on the robe. [The meat, and fat, scraped from robes, or other skins, are called "fleshings."]

"Grandmother talked to the little bird, and finally after its belly was full the chickadee said, 'Leave your work for a while, and follow me. I wish to talk to you over yonder by that creek. Get somebody to take care of your little girl, and meet me at the creek.'

"Grandmother ran to her lodge, got a woman friend to care for the little girl, who became my mother, took a sweat-bath, put on her finest clothes, and went to the creek."

These "sweat-baths" were taken in tiny, conical, willow lodges, covered tightly with buffalo robes. Heated stones were rolled inside, and freely sprinkled with water, the resultant vapor thoroughly cleansing the occupant's body. The "sweat-bath" was severe, and when taken before or after a "medicine-dream," was symbolic of mental purification.

"At first grandmother did not see the chickadee. She could hear the bird talking and laughing to itself, but could not see it until it came to sit on a willow right above her head. 'Look,' it said, going up into the air, flying higher and higher. Straight up it went, growing larger and larger and larger, until it was as large as a war-eagle [mountain, or golden eagle]. 'See,' it called down to my grandmother, 'there is great power in little things.' And then my grandmother saw that the bird held a buffalo calf in each of its taloned feet. 'I am a woman, as you are. Like you I have to work, and make the best of this life,' said the bird. 'I am your friend, and yet to help you I must first hurt you. You will have three sons, but will lose two of them. One will live to be a good man. You must never eat eggs, never. Have you listened?' asked the bird, settling down again, and growing small.

" 'Yes, I have listened,' my grandmother told that chickadee, and from that day she never ate an egg. But her children did, and her man, my grandfather, did. They would not listen. Two of her boys, and her man, my grandfather, were killed by Lacota. It is bad to harm the chickadee, and foolish not to listen to him," she finished, emphatically.

THIRTEEN

All that night the wind howled like a pack of buffalo wolves, rattling the dry tops of the Agency cottonwoods until daybreak. When, in the gray light, I reached from my bed to rescue my shoes from a pile of powdery snow that had been driven through my open window, a solitary coyote was wailing, his voice sounding tame after the blizzard. The plains were white with snow and the thermometer standing at zero, when I went to the schoolhouse to get a fire going in the cannon stove before the women came. Somebody, in the night, had sought shelter from the storm here. The messy little cupboard on the wall had been visited. Its paper bags had been clumsily opened, dashes of their contents littering the shelves. A trickle of sugar that had fallen to the floor gritted beneath my feet. The little cookstove, its pipe connected to the vent of the cannon heater, had been used. The box of matches on the cupboard's top had contributed to somebody's pocket. Whoever had been here had had a fire; and he had been a white man. I knew this by a heel track left in the ashes scattered upon the floor.

But now his fire was out, dead; a tin cup of water, standing on the hearth of the stove, was frozen solid.

The windows were rattling annoyingly. I wedged their sashes with folded paper torn from a seed catalogue, wondering if the bluebirds, recently returned from the southland, had survived the storm. Outside, the snow was drifting into little dry piles with sharpened ends, all pointing one way, to the north. An ancient Ford, its radiator steaming white, went rattling by, a section of its ragged top whipping about like a tattered flag.

"This isn't a very good day for rattlesnakes," I said when Pretty-shield and Goes-together entered to stand by the stove, their blankets drawn tightly over their chins. "What did you do when people were bitten by rattlesnakes, Pretty-shield?" I asked when we had taken our places beside the table.

"A rattlesnake wouldn't bother anybody today," she laughed. Then, after arranging her blanket, "Rattlesnakes gave us little trouble. I can remember but three people who were bitten by them. None died.

"Once, in the moon that plums fall [September] seven of us women were on Warm-water [Soap creek] gathering plums. The little trees grew plentifully along the Warm-water where it came out onto the plains, and their plums reddened the ground. Be-

162

sides the plums, many leaves had fallen, and these leaves covered many plums, so that they could not be seen. But we knew they were there, and after spreading buffalo robes we began raking the hidden plums into them, with a good many leaves. None of us noticed where we were putting our hands, while we talked and laughed and raked in the plums, until one of the women screamed. A rattlesnake was hidden in the plum leaves."

Here Goes-together, who had grown tense, jumped as though she herself had been bitten, nearly upsetting the table. Pretty-shield, now convulsed with laughter, had suddenly reached down and pinched the interpreter's leg. Several minutes elapsed before Pretty-shield could control her mirth.

"Yes, the snake bit the woman's finger," she began again, still chuckling at the nervous interpreter. "The woman pulled her knife from its scabbard and cut off the snake's head," she went on, with merry glances.

"I ran to her, and so did my aunt. We tied the woman's arm above the hand a little, and twisted hard. But the hand and arm began at once to swell badly. The woman was not herself. Her eyes grew glittery. Her tongue darted out, and back into her mouth, like a snake's. My aunt sent a young woman for some mint that grew everywhere along the water, and when she brought it, my aunt chewed some of the mint and then spat it into the woman's face and upon her hand and arm. I saw my aunt pick out the snake's fang from the wounded hand. It was like a needle. My aunt sang her medicine-song and the woman got well.

"And another time," she went on, "a woman, whose name was Cat-tails, was bitten by a rattlesnake while graining a buffalo robe that was pegged to the ground. She dropped her scraper, and when she reached to pick it up a snake bit her hand. She jumped upon the snake and held it, calling for help, while the snake coiled itself around her leg, until a man came and killed the snake for her. Her arm was swollen so large that they had to cut her dress away from it.

"Her father sent for Good-otter, a wise-one, giving her two horses to help Cat-tails. But Good-otter could not save all the woman's fingers, and said so at the beginning. She used an otter's skin, making it act as a snake does. Almost at once the wound began to discharge, the swelling to go down, and then the snake's fang fell out of the wounded finger. But Cat-tails lost that finger, as Good-otter had said.

"Then there was another," Pretty-shield continued, with a quick glance at Goes-together who had now steeled herself against jumping. "This was but a few years ago, not more than twenty-five. A little girl,

who had gone swimming with some others, was returning to the Crow camp. The trail that she was
following was dusty. She was scuffing her feet in this
dust when a rattlesnake bit her foot. Her grandfather carried the little girl to a white doctor's place
but the doctor was gone, so that the old man called
Goes-ahead and me. The little girl got well. In four
days she was as good as ever. There are but two moons
when rattlesnakes are bad. During these two moons
[August and September] they cannot see; they strike
because of this, strike to save themselves from being
stepped upon. If they could see they would run away,"
she finished, moving nearer to the stove.

I put coal on the fire. "Now tell me your medicine-
dream," I said, moving the table nearer her.

"I had lost a little girl, a beautiful baby girl," she
said. "I had been mourning for more than two moons.
I had slept little, sometimes lying down alone in the
hills at night, and always on hard places. I ate only
enough to keep me alive, hoping for a medicine-
dream, a vision, that would help me to live and to
help others. One morning, after a night spent on a
high cliff, when I was returning to my lodge to pack
things for a long move, I saw a woman ahead of me.
She was walking fast, as though she hoped to reach
my lodge before I could get there. But suddenly she

stopped and stood still, looking down at the ground. I thought I knew her, thought that she was a woman who had died four years before. I felt afraid. I stopped, my heart beating fast. 'Come here, daughter.' Her words seemed to draw me toward her against my will.

"Walking a few steps I saw that she was not a real woman, but that she was a Person [apparition], and that she was standing beside an ant hill.

" 'Come here, daughter.' Again I walked toward her when I did not wish to move. Stopping by her side, I did not try to look into her face. My heart was nearly choking me. 'Rake up the edges of this ant hill and ask for the things that you wish, daughter,' the Person said; and then she was gone. Only the ant hill was there; and a wind was blowing. I saw the grass tremble, as I was trembling, when I raked up the edges of the ant hill, as the Person had told me. Then I made my wish, 'Give me good luck, and a good life,' I said aloud, looking at the hills.

"I was weak. In my lodge there were no bed-robes for me, because I had long ago destroyed all my comfortable things. But now, in this medicine-dream, I entered a beautiful white lodge, with a war-eagle at the head. He did not speak to me, and yet I have often seen him since that day. And even now the ants help me. I listen to them always. They are my medicine, these busy, powerful little people, the ants."

FOURTEEN

"OF course the Lacota, Striped-feathered-arrows [Cheyenne], Arapahoes, Pecunnies, and other tribes never let us rest, so that there was always war. When our enemies were not bothering *us*, our warriors were bothering *them*, so there was always fighting going on somewhere. We women sometimes tried to keep our men from going to war, but this was like talking to winter-winds; and of course there was always some woman, sometimes many women, mourning for men who had been killed in war. These women had to be taken care of. Somebody had to kill meat for them. Their fathers or uncles or brothers did this until the women married again, which they did not always do, so that war made more work for everybody. There were few lazy ones among us in those days. My people used to be too proud to be lazy. Besides this, in the old days a lazy person didn't get along very well, man or woman."

"Were there always men left in your camps?" I asked, hoping that the answer might remind her of another story.

"Yes," she said, "but sometimes when war-parties

were out looking for the enemy, and besides these, many hunters were on the plains after buffalo, only old men were left in camp, old ones, and a few lazy young ones. Once, a long time ago, the Lacota nearly wiped the Crows out, because all the men were gone to steal horses. Nearly all the women were killed, and all the old men that had been left in the village, besides. But this was long before my time. Even in my days young men were always going to war, or to steal horses, leaving the village short of warriors, because they could not marry until they had counted coup, or had reached the age of twenty-five years. Young men do not like to wait so long," she smiled.

"My man, Goes-ahead, was a Fox [member of that secret society] and although we women had no secret societies we sided with our men, so that my heart was always strong for the Foxes. The Foxes were warlike. We women did not like war, and yet we could not help it, because our men loved war. Always there was some man missing, and always some woman was having to go and live with her relatives, because women are not hunters. And then there were the orphans that war made. They had to be cared for by somebody. You see that when we women lost our men we lost our own, and our children's, living. I am glad that war has gone forever. It was no good—*no good!*"

Here her signs were most emphatic.

"I want to go back to the time when I was eight years old," said Pretty-shield. "Will it be all right to do this now, after we have passed that time?"

"Yes, always when you think of a story of your girlhood I wish you would tell it."

"Well, once when we had much fat meat that had been roasted in meat-holes, and were almost lazy from eating, our village moved a long way. My mother and I let the travois go on ahead of us, because we saw some roots that we wished to dig."

Meat was often roasted in holes in the ground, hot stones being used in very much the same way as in fireless cookers of modern days.

"When at last my mother and I started to follow the people we were alone on the wide plains. My mother was riding a mare that had a colt. This colt kept lagging back, sometimes getting far behind, making the mare so nervous that she kept trying to turn around. Her whinnying made a lot of noise, and we did not like to hear it, because we were alone. At last the troublesome colt got so far behind that we had to turn back to find it. When we found it the colt wanted to nurse, but we were so far behind now that my mother would not wait for the colt to fill up. I have often wondered what might have happened to us if she had waited for that little colt to nurse," Pretty-shield said speculatively. "We might have saved ourselves a lot of trouble, and yet we might have been captured by the Lacota and enslaved.

"We were riding fast, my mother ahead and I behind, with the bothersome colt between us, when we saw Lacota coming. My heart fell to the ground. We both forgot all about the colt. Mother turned up a deep coulee, with me by her side. 'They may not have seen us,' she said, lashing her old mare that was going like the wind.

"But I thought they must have seen us. A hundred warriors with two hundred eyes must have seen as much as we two women saw with but four eyes, I felt sure.

"We began to go up hill, our horses getting slower and slower, until at last we reached the top. Here my mother stopped and got down. Her mare was breathing so fast that her sides were going in and out like a tired wolf's. We had stopped behind a juniper tree and my mother, keeping behind it, looked back. Then she called me. I got down, and went to her. 'Look,' she pointed.

"The Lacota had found the place where we had turned away from the trail the travois had made. Four of them, afoot, were following our tracks. I knew what this meant. A party of Lacota would take up our trail and ride us down.

"My mother saw that I understood. 'Daughter,' she said, softly, putting her arm around me, 'we have not always *lived* together, but before this sun touches the world we may *die* together.'

"She tightened my saddle's cinch, and that of her own. Then she took a fine wolf's skin from her saddle, and brushed the ground with it, as though wiping away our horses' tracks. 'If they come to this place they will be fooled by this,' she told me. But I was afraid.

" 'Come,' she said; and we rode again. There were two creeks far ahead of us now. Mother headed for the one that was on our left a little, singing her medicine-song, 'I'm doing as you told me to do; I'm doing as you told me to do.'

"Suddenly our horses told us that there was something bad ahead. My mother stopped so quickly that I ran against her. She put the wolf skin over her head and sang, 'I'm doing as you told me to do; I'm doing as you told me to do.'

"A black cloud, full of thunder that sounded like many guns shooting together near my ears, passed over our heads. I felt a strong wind on my shoulders.

The black cloud ran back to hang over the Lacota, its thunders nearly bursting my ears.

" 'Ho!' cried my mother, above the wind. And away we dashed again. When we came out of the wind I could hear my mother's voice singing her medicine-song.

"We got away. That wolf skin was big medicine. I have it to this day," she finished, confidentially.

"Did the Lacota attack the Crow village?" I asked.

"No," she answered. "Our warriors went out to find the Lacota. But I do not like to talk of war. The last time I did I nearly forgot my grandchildren."

"Did the Crow warriors find the Lacota?" I pressed her.

"Yes. Next morning there were many Lacota horses mixed with ours, and I saw more Lacota scalps than I had ever before seen at one time. No Crow had been killed, and but one warrior wounded. His name was Blue-scalp. We won a big fight that time. The men had a big dance, with their faces painted black [sign of victory].

"But it was not long until the Lacota got even with us. This was always the way with our wars. No matter which side won a battle, ourselves or our enemies, the loser always got even in the end. Getting even was what kept our men fighting; and this wanting to get even was what made so much mourning, too."

"Tell me about captive women, slave-women," I said, to lead her away from her disconcerting thoughts. "Did the Crows capture many women?"

"Yes," she answered, "even in my time. And because they were treated well they never tried to get away. They had the same rights as Crow women, and worked no harder."

I saw that she was inclined to drop this subject, and so pressed her. "Did the Lacota often capture Crow women?" I asked.

"Oh, yes, but they nearly always got away and came home, because they were treated badly. If they were pretty, our men sometimes married Lacota and Pecunnie women who had been captured. Perhaps this was good, since it brought us new blood, and yet I did not like to see our blood mixed with others. I am a pure-blooded Crow woman, myself, and have always been strong and healthy."

"Tell me a story about a slave-woman," I urged.

"I will tell you about Feather-woman, a Lacota who, with one hundred other Lacota women, was brought to our village by a large war-party of Crows.

"One hundred women, seated in a circle, even though they may all be pretty, make men think of the meat that will be needed to feed so many," she smiled, broadly.

"Our chief called upon our men to take one slave apiece, as far as they would go; and in a little while the big circle of Lacota women had melted away like snow in the springtime. But the Lacota men missed these women. Yes, because a lodge is not a very good place for a man when there is no woman in it; they missed these women. These Lacota men did not like to think of living always alone, and so they did something about it.

"One day a Crow wolf saw a Lacota standing on the top of a high hill on the plains. The Lacota spoke, by signs, to the Crow, saying that he would like to talk to the Crows in council, that he had something to say there.

"The Crow wolf, answering the Lacota in signs, told him to go to the chief's lodge. 'You will know it by the medicine-pipe that is tied over its door. Take down this pipe, hold it in your hands, and enter the lodge. You will be safe,' he said.

"The Lacota slipped carefully into the Crow village, being afraid, until he held the medicine-pipe in his hands. Then, knowing that he was safe, he entered the chief's lodge, where he was given meat to eat, and some berries. When he had eaten, our chief asked him, in signs, why he had come.

" 'When I was a small boy I lived two years with your people,' answered the Lacota, speaking Crow. 'I liked the Crows so much that after I got back to my own people I missed my Crow friends. Now I have come here to ask you to let us have our women. We need them, and will give you good horses and fine clothing for them. Will you listen?'

" 'Yes, I will listen,' our chief answered. 'But before•I tell you that you may have your women I must talk to my warriors. They must agree, or the women will have to stay here.'

"A crier rode through the village, spreading the news. Quickly the warriors gathered to hear what the Lacota had to say. 'It is good,' they told him, thinking of the meat they had to kill to feed the hundred slave-women, when they had plenty of women of their own blood to take care of.

" 'It is good, then,' said Silver-tip, our chief, 'but let no Lacota come here unless he has a woman in our village. One hundred men may come after these women, and no more. Ho!'

"On the tenth day after this our wolves signaled 'The enemy is coming.' But even before this signal came our warriors were ready for battle, because they knew that the Lacota might lie, that more than one hundred might come, with getting back their women as an excuse to get near our village.

"More than two hundred warriors rode out to meet the Lacota, ready for a fight; but this time the Lacota had not lied. They had come, one hundred of them, to get their women, and not to fight. Some of our men who had lost fathers and brothers at the hands of the Lacota were ugly. They came near forgetting that the Lacota were visitors. Silver-tip, our chief, warned these men of punishment if they did not behave themselves. This quieted them, so that when the Lacota who had promised to come after the women, spoke, they listened to him.

"He carried the pipe [was leader] for the Lacota, and upon reaching our village he walked straight to Silver-tip, asking him if he would lay his medicine-pipe beside his on the ground, before all the people.

"When the two pipes were side by side on the ground before all the people the Lacota piled fine shirts, and leggings, and moccasins, and parfleches, high about them. One Lacota, wearing beautiful clothes, rode up to the circle of slave-women who had been seated on the ground, and gave his clothes and four fine horses for his woman. One by one these slave-women were taken; all but one of them, and this one was Feather-woman.

"During all this time she had sat a little apart in the circle, with her head covered, as though ashamed. No Lacota asked for her. I felt sorry to see her there, alone, one out of the hundred. I wondered why no man had asked for her. Finally a Lacota woman, the only one in the party, walked up to Feather-woman, leading a little girl by the hand. I could not understand the words that this woman spoke to Feather-woman, but saw her give her the little girl and then go away.

"Feather-woman uncovered her head, took the little girl in her arms, and then again lifting up her robe, covered the little girl's head and her own. They were both crying beneath the robe.

" 'This woman will not be chosen,' I heard the Lacota, who spoke Crow, say in a loud voice. 'She killed her own man. She is a wicked one. Nobody wants her.'

"Feather-woman must have understood the Lacota's Crow words. I saw her bend lower, saw the robe shake with her sobbing, until finally a Crow woman led her away.

"And now in our village the Lacota made peace, promising to go beyond The-big-tree and stay there. This big tree was on the Platte river. It may be there to this day. I do not know. White men cut down such trees, and it may be gone. I cannot make you know just where it stood; but it took several buffalo robes to reach around it, and everybody knew where it was, what tree was meant when we said 'The-big-tree,' so that the Lacota understood. But of course they forgot about their promise. They came into our country many times after this, sometimes to their sorrow," she said grimly.

"Once I hated the Lacota, and nothing else. Now I hate nobody, nothing. But I must tell you more about Feather-woman. Both she and her daughter, whose name was Comes-herself, died here with my people, the Crows.

"The Lacota who spoke Crow had said that Feather-woman was a wicked one. And she *had* been wicked. But now, after the Lacota would not take her back with them, she began to be a different woman. She walked with her little girl on her back whenever the Crows moved their village. She fasted, walked the hills alone at night, looking for Helpers, until everybody pitied her. She grew thin from not eating, and yet she kept her little girl well fed, carrying her on her back wherever she went.

"One night when Feather-woman was out on the hills she put her little girl into a hole in the rocks, and then sat outside to watch for Helpers. A mountain-lion came to her, said that he knew she was sorry for what she had done, and promised to help her if she would promise to be always kind to others.

"The next day, while Feather-woman, afoot, with her child on her back, was following the travois, one of the bravest and best men in the Crow tribe asked her to come, as his sister, and live with him and his woman. His name was Two-faces. He and his woman had no children of their own, so that Feather-woman and her little girl now had a good home. She became great. Her medicine, the mountain-lion, always helped her. She was one of the kindest women I have ever known. Once I saw her heal a sick woman by touching her with her hand. She even helped Two-faces, taught him how to make other people do as he wished by looking at them. Two-faces kept this power until he died, because he was always a good man. But Feather-woman finally forgot her promise to the mountain-lion to be kind. She lost her power, and was killed by her own people in the snow when Fort C. F. Smith was being built [1866]. Her daughter, Comes-herself, died two snows ago.

"I must go now," she said, rising. "After I feed my grandchildren I will come back and tell you about some Crow slave-women who got away from the Lacota."

179

FIFTEEN

Leaving the building I passed Old Smoky, the aged Negro errand-runner for the Agency. Far from his kind, almost a tradition now, Smoky has been at "Crow" for a lifetime, having come here as a servant to an officer in the United States Army. Shuffling as only an aged Negro can, Old Smoky was playing "Listen to the Mocking Bird" on a mouth organ pressed to his thick lips with one claw-like hand, while the other grudgingly pushed a high-wheeled cart toward the Agency Postoffice. He bowed

deferentially, but without missing a note of the air he must have learned when a boy. I remembered having heard a story of his arrest, for some alleged crime, long ago.

I believe that it was General Hugh L. Scott who made the arrest. However, Old Smoky does not like to discuss the affair. "No, suh, Boss, I ain't nevah been arrested," he insists. "De Gineral done arrest a man dat was *wiv* me, fo' something er othah. Dat's all, suh, dat's all."

Before returning to our room I went to the Trader's store for some silver money. Coming out I met Pretty-shield on her way back to the school building. "The wind is cold," I said in signs.

"Yes," she answered, walking beside me till, hearing wailing behind us, she turned just as a tiny child seized her skirt, crying pitifully.

"Tst, tst, tst!" Pretty-shield lifted the child to her arms. "No coot! Me—" Then, despairing of her ability to make me understand the situation in her pidgin English, she set the screaming child upon its feet. "I will take her to my place. I will come back fast," she signed.

"Good!" I answered, watching the faithful old woman hurry away with the now quiet child in her arms. "Another grandchild," I thought.

Goes-together and I had not long to wait, however. Pretty-shield, out of breath from running, came in laughing merrily. "I'm no good," she signed. "My breath is short. I am old. That was my grand-daughter that made me go back to my place."

Then, sitting down, she wiped her perspiring forehead with her blanket, and took up her story telling, still panting a little from her exertion. I thought how different she was from the Crow men, in her anxiety to keep her engagements. I had spent hours, days, waiting for the men, but scarcely a minute waiting for Pretty-shield, who has two families of grandchildren to care for. She made me her friend by her honest earnestness and her love for her grandchildren, who were constantly in her thoughts. Since coming home to write her story I have sent her enough deer skins to make them moccasins for a year, at least.

"I had an aunt who was captured by the Lacota," Pretty-shield began, "but she got away, and again reached her people, the Crows. I am not going to tell about her, but about another Crow woman who escaped from the Lacota, because this one had some strange things happen to her before she finally got back to the Crow village. My grandmother knew her, and told me her story when I was yet a little girl. It begins with a boy, though," with a quick glance at me.

"One day in the fall when lodge-fires burn nearly all the time, a boy playing with some other boys was chased into his mother's lodge. The lodges in those days were small, the distance between the door and the lodge-fire being short. This boy, in his hurry to get away from his pursuers, stumbled in the doorway, falling with his face in the lodge-fire. His face was so badly burned that he knew he would be scarred for life. He felt ashamed to meet his boy friends again. That night he stole away and did not return. He was eleven years old.

"Many snows came and went away again, without anybody seeing this boy. And then one day the Lacota captured eighteen Crow women who were picking berries. One of these Crow women had a young daughter with her, and these two began planning to escape almost as soon as they reached the Lacota village, which was on a creek in the plains, and in a cottonwood grove.

"Each afternoon when they were sent to gather and bring in wood from the grove they hid a little pemmican, saved from their meals or stolen from the parfleches. One afternoon, before they had cached much pemmican, all the men were out on the plains running buffalo. Here was a good chance for the woman and her young daughter to get away.

"Pretending to go after wood, the two went to the grove as usual, but instead of returning with wood on their backs, they raised their cache of pemmican and fled, following the creek that ran through the cottonwood grove. This creek came to the plains from far-off mountains. Willows and cottonwood trees and ash trees and box-elder trees grew thickly along its banks, so that the woman and her young daughter could not be seen from the plains. They ran fast until night came, then they traveled slowly, but did not stop to rest until at last they reached the mountains.

"On the third day, when they were high up on the hills, they saw the Lacota, in two parties, looking for them. This made them go even higher up on the mountains, where the way was difficult, and yet they did not come down to the plains for four days. On the fourth day they worked their way down a creek toward the plains, hoping to find some turnips. Both had knives, and the woman had made herself a root-digger, so that when they came to a patch of turnips she began to dig them.

" 'Ahh, see, mother.' The young daughter pointed to fresh digging. 'A white bear is here. I am afraid.'

" 'Yes, he is digging turnips,' said the woman, look-ing at the fresh digging. 'But do not be afraid. The animals often help people who are in trouble. Per-haps this bear-person will help us. Let us go on down this creek to the plains.'

"The creek came to a flat place where there were great trees and thick bushes. Here, as though it did not wish to go out into the hot sunshine of the plains, the water lingered, lazily, making deep pools in shady places. And here, because the water was cool, the woman and her young daughter knelt down to drink.

" 'Ahh, mother, see! Here in the mud is a track of the white bear. I am afraid.'

" 'Shhh! Do not say that,' cautioned the woman.

185

'He may be helping us even now. Speak no words against him, daughter. Do not even *think* such words. Drink, and then we will travel again.'

"When darkness came they stopped on a ledge of rock in the foothills. Their pemmican was gone. They had eaten nothing excepting a few turnips, for two whole days and nights. Both were tired, both hungry, and both went to sleep on the rock.

"In the night the woman wakened, and sitting up called softly for Helpers. But no Person answered. There was nothing in sight excepting the stars when she again laid herself down on the rock. She slept.

"The day was showing a little when, wakening, the woman thought that her legs felt strangely warm. Reaching down with her hand she felt *hair*. The white bear was lying with his side against her legs!

"She did not cry out, did not speak, did not even move her legs until, just when the northern sky began to brighten, the white bear stood up, stretching himself, as a person does who has been long asleep, and said: 'I am going now. You had better follow me. Travel in *that* direction,' he pointed. 'I will wait for you at The-wide-willows on Tongue river. Remember my words.'

"The woman sat up, saw the white bear disappear in the direction that he had told her to follow, and then called her daughter. The sky in the east was getting yellow.

"They traveled, digging roots now and then, till they reached The-wide-willows on the Tongue river. Even before they reached this place they saw the white bear. He was digging roots on a hillside; and besides this they saw that he had killed a young buffalo cow. He had eaten the front quarters, leaving the rest, as though he knew that the woman and her young daughter would want it. The woman's daughter, being very hungry, wished to eat some of it at once.

" 'Wait until I first ask the bear if we may have the meat,' said the woman. 'Stay here. I will go to him alone.'

" 'Yes, of course, the meat is for you and your young daughter,' said the white bear. And he even sat up to watch them eat, but did not come very near.

"When they had eaten their meal the woman cut all the meat that she thought she could carry into thin strips, and spread them upon sticks laid on the ground, so that when the day came again the sun would dry the meat, making it lighter to carry. She let the sun dry the meat for four days. Then, while she was making it into a pack, the bear came to her.

'Travel in *that* direction,' he pointed. Then, after the woman and her young daughter had started, he called, 'I will see you again four days from now, near the Bighorn river!'

"The woman and her daughter were rested now, and having soled their moccasins with the cow's hide, they could travel faster. They reached the Bighorn river early on the fourth day, and of course the woman began at once to look for her Helper, the white bear. He was nowhere in sight. Not until the sun was nearly down to the world did the woman see him; and then he signed to her to come alone to him to hear what he had to say.

" 'I have been high up on the Bighorn mountains,' the bear told her when they were alone together on a high hill. 'I have seen the whole country, and there is a great flood. The rivers have grown too large. They have had to spread out over the land, and your people have moved away from the water. You will have to wait four years before you can go to them. Come, I will show you that I have spoken with a straight tongue [not lied].'

"On a high mountain the bear lifted the woman above his head. She saw the Crow country flooded with water, as the bear had told her, and now she began to cry. 'Ah, what can I do?' she sobbed.

" 'I saw a man on that mountain over there,' said the bear, pointing with his paw. 'You and your young daughter had better find him. He is a Crow, and ought to help you. I cannot stay around here much longer. I have a woman and children, and must go back to the country that I left when I began to help you. Go, you and your daughter, to that mountain, and look for that man. I may see you again.'

"When the bear had gone, and the woman found herself alone on that mountain, she felt afraid. She sat down and cried. But the bear, even if he heard her, did not come back, and at last, after night came, she got up and went to her young daughter.

"In the morning they began to climb the mountain, as the bear had advised. By the time the sun had reached the middle of the sky on the second day they came to the rim of The-black-canyon, and looked down. By the time the sun had gone behind the high mountain, and The-black-canyon began to look darker, its bottom farther away, the woman had made a bed of ground-cedar for her daughter. But she herself did not try to sleep. All through the night she walked and cried aloud for Helpers. The-black-canyon and the winds made strange noises there. These kept her afraid.

"When the first light of morning touched the rim

189

of The-black-canyon she saw a man walking there, walking on the rim of The-black-canyon, on the far side; and the man had a heavy pack on his back. He seemed not to know that he walked so near the edge, not to feel the great pack on his back that the woman could now see was a whole bull-elk! He did not stagger beneath his load, did not even look across the deep canyon. He kept traveling along its rim until he was out of sight.

"Now the woman called her daughter; and then they both saw the man coming toward them on their side of the canyon. Fear nearly stopped their hearts. On he came as though there were no pack on his back, the two women shivering with fear, until he reached a smooth rock not far from them. Here he stopped, letting the bull-elk fall to the ground beside it. Without speaking, without even looking at the women, he cut off the elk's hindquarters, shouldered the rest, as though it were nothing at all—and then stepped off the canyon's rim *into the air that was streaked with sunlight.*

"The woman and her daughter ran to the rim and looked down. But the sun had not yet reached so far as the canyon's bottom. They could see nothing below the line of morning light that was not yet half way down. They could hear nothing except the wind among the rocks. And yet, while the sun climbed higher and higher, the woman and her young daughter kept looking down into The-black-canyon. They were looking when the sun was in the middle of the sky; but they saw nobody, nothing, on the bottom, except rocks.

" 'Did you see his face?' the woman asked her daughter, finally, when they had grown hungry.

" 'No. I was too much afraid,' said the young daughter. 'He is such a strong man, mother. Who can he be?'

" 'I do not know,' the woman answered. She had seen the man's face. It was so badly scarred that it had terrified her.

" 'I will look for some water, and then we will eat some of our dried meat,' she told her daughter. But there was no water on the mountain-top. Far down in The-black-canyon there was water. The woman could hear it running over rocks, and yet could find no place to go down to it. She had given up, had turned back, when she saw water in a dish-like rock, enough to last them for two days. Rain had not fallen for more than a moon, and yet here was water in the rock. They drank of it; and each night more water came to the dish-like rock, as though it were fed by a spring; and yet there was no spring there.

"On the fourth morning the man came to them. 'I am Lost-boy, the one who fell into the lodge-fire,' he said, turning away his face that was terrible to see. 'Come down into The-black-canyon and live as my neighbors. I will kill your meat for you, will help you. I am a Crow. Come down,' he finished, stepping off The-black-canyon's rim into the thin air, as before.

"The woman, after searching for four days, found a way to go down. The man was there, waiting for them. But there was no lodge in sight, nothing except the rushing creek and the smooth sides of The-black-canyon.

" 'I live in here,' the man pointed to the hard rock. 'But you women will need a lodge to live in. Here are skins enough,' he said, pointing to a pile of elk hides, 'and my people will bring you lodge-poles. I am going to rest now,' he finished, disappearing into the smooth wall of The-black-canyon so quickly that they did not see him go away.

"The woman and her young daughter were badly frightened. In front of them was the high, smooth side of The-black-canyon, behind them the roaring white water of a creek, and over their heads, far, far up, only the sky that was like a narrow strip of blue paint. The winds blew in their faces, and a mist from the white water dampened their hair.

"'Ahh!' The young daughter took hold of her mother's arm. 'See,' she pointed, her hand trembling.

"The-little-people, many, many of them, were coming along the white water of the creek, and even down the smooth sides of The-black-canyon; and they were carrying lodge-poles that were nearly as large around as themselves!

"The woman and her daughter were standing on a wide ledge that was flat and as smooth as the canyon's walls. There was no place to hide, and besides there was not time. The-little-people, some of them carrying long lodge-poles, some dragging them, reached the flat ledge in no time at all. Without speaking, or even seeing the women, The-little-people piled their poles on the flat ledge, and then walked into the wall of The-black-canyon, leaving the woman and her young daughter there, with the wind blowing their hair.

"When the woman and her daughter had made their lodge the woman said, 'The man who has all this great power is a Crow. I know his mother. Go in there. Be his woman, and then we shall be safe from all harm.'

"The daughter watched for a chance to enter the wall of The-black-canyon. She knew that she could not go into it until the man *let* her in, so she watched until he came out. Then, when he again went in, she followed, lying down inside near the door. But he sent her out. Three times she did this thing, and three times the man sent her out of his lodge. But when she went in the fourth time the man saw that she was brave, and took her as his woman.

"When the fourth snow came, and the man and his woman had a son, the Crows found them. It was this way that it happened: The man was out hunting elk. Some Crow hunters who were in the mountains saw him carrying an elk on his shoulder, and followed him to The-black-canyon. 'No man can do such a thing as this,' they said, wondering at the man's strength. When they saw him go into the wall of The-black-canyon they were afraid, and ran away.

"These Crow hunters told their story in the village. Other warriors, who listened, one of them the old father of the lost boy, went to The-black-canyon, where he waited for the man to come out of the wall. When, early one morning, the man appeared on the rim of the canyon the father of Lost-boy recognized him. 'My son! My son!' he called, loudly.

"The man came to him, took him to his lodge in the wall of The-black-canyon, showed him his son and his woman and his mother-in-law, who lived in a lodge outside. And to please his old father he finally brought his son and his woman and his mother-in-law back to the Crow people, where they lived until they died of old age.

"The man, Lost-boy, told the Crows that he had lived in the rock with The-little-people ever since the day after he had burned his face. The-little-people gave Lost-boy a big medicine. He became a great healer of wounds. I did not know him, myself, but my grandmother did."

SIXTEEN

"No," she said, in answer to my question, "I never did anything to help a slave-woman, because when we had slaves I was too young to help anybody. In late years I have cooked and worked hard for Lacota and Cheyenne visitors, the very people who were our worst enemies; and they gave me presents when they went away. Shall I tell you about that?" she asked, as though she could think of nothing else.

"What was your people's opinion of Sitting-bull, the Lacota chief? Did they believe him to be a great man?" I asked.

My question pleased her. "Wait," she signed, pressing her clenched hand against her scarred forehead. "Ahh! I was about twenty-eight," she began, her eyes again merry. "Yes, I was about twenty-eight or thirty years old when I saw Sitting-bull here at this very place. I will tell you what happened on that day, and then you may write down your own answers to your own questions.

"There was peace between my people and the Lacota. One day in the summertime Sitting-bull, with many of his people, came here to visit us. There was much feasting and dancing and many talks during the four days of visiting with our old enemies. On the fourth day, when the Crows were going to give many horses to our Lacota visitors, the people all formed a great circle. Sitting-bull, wearing beautiful clothes, walked to its center, and sat down there, with a rifle across his knees. To me he seemed proud. He did not even look at the people around him. While I was thinking these things Crazy-head, one of our chiefs, rode into the circle with several horses that he intended giving to the Lacota. He began to speak. His words made me feel afraid. He said, 'I love my people, all of them. I now ask them to listen, and to use their eyes. We have to give each visiting Lacota a good horse, but before we do this I am going to show you what kind of a man this great Lacota chief is; and I am also going to show you what a man ought to be. This Lacota calls himself great, and yet, if what I have often heard is true, he is not kind to his people. A brave man is seldom unkind. Let us see if Sitting-bull is brave.'

"My heart was in my mouth when Crazy-head finished speaking. Turning his horse he rode around the circle, around Sitting-bull, who yet sat on the ground, as though he had heard nothing; and perhaps did not hear, since Crazy-head spoke in the Crow language. But there were Lacota there who knew our tongue, and I felt afraid that there would be war.

"Crazy-head carried no gun, not even a knife. His face was painted with white clay [paint of the buffalo-bull]. In his hand he carried the tail of a buffalo that had an eagle's feather on it. He called an interpreter, a Crow who could speak the Lacota language, and then, riding up to Sitting-bull, Crazy-head got down from his horse.

" 'How can a man who thinks himself great be unkind to his people?' he asked Sitting-bull. 'I have killed more than one of your people. I have even counted more than one coup on them. This is how I counted one of my coups in a fight with your people near the spot now occupied by the white man's town of Cody. *You* were there. I saw you there.'

"Springing to his side, Crazy-head seized Sitting-bull's rifle, took it from him, and tossed it into the crowd. I saw Onions, a son of Crazy-head's, pick it up.

"And this was not all. Crazy-head pushed Sitting-bull over on his back, and then jumped across him. 'These are some of the things I did that day when I fought your people, when I counted a coup on a

Lacota warrior, the day that you were there. I *saw* you there. Ho!' he said; and then all the Crows gave the war-cry, 'Whooooooo!'

"The Lacota women were afraid; but the men of the Lacota only laughed at Sitting-bull. They did not love him. They feared his medicine, but did not respect him. Sitting-bull possessed a great power, a power that might have made his people love him; but he abused it, and so lost it. His own people did not love him.

"Now, if you have written the answers to your own questions I will go to my place. I will come back when I have fed my grandchildren," she finished, hurrying to the door.

I had not expected Pretty-shield to be enthusiastic about Sitting-bull's prowess as a warrior, and yet her story surprised me. It is written as she told it. However it must be understood that the Crow chief, Crazy-head, used only the time-honored custom of recounting his coup to insult Sitting-bull in the presence of both his own people and the visiting Lacota [Sioux].

"Shall I tell you, Sign-talker," Pretty-shield went on when she returned, "how a fight between the Crows and the Lacota was won by a woman?"

Eagerly I assented.

"Once, when I was eight years old, we moved our village from The-mountain-lion's-lodge [Pompey's Pillar] to the place where the white man's town of Huntley now stands. There were not many of us in this band. Sixteen men were with us when the women began to set up their lodges, and one man named Covered-with-grass was sent out as a wolf. I could see him on the hill when my mother was setting up her lodge-poles. I was dragging the poles of my play-lodge to a nice place that I had selected when I saw Covered-with-grass, the wolf on the hill, signal, 'The enemy is coming.'

"Instantly two men leaped upon the backs of horses, their war-horses, that were always kept tied near lodges, and rode out on the plains to drive the other horses into camp.

"There was great excitement, much running about by the women, who left their lodges just as they happened to be when the signal came. Some of the lodges had but a few poles up. Others, whose owners were quicker, had their lodge-skins tied, hanging loosely from the skin-poles.

"Men, watching the hills, stationed themselves, one between every two lodges. Mothers, piling packs and parfleches into breast-works, called their children; and horses whinnied. Then I saw the horses that had been out on the plains coming fast, their hoofs making a great noise and much dust. I must get out of the way.

"Dragging my poles, a load beneath each arm, I ran between two lodges whose lodge-skins were flapping in the wind, my own little lodge yet on my back. In came the horses, more than a hundred, sweeping into the camp between two lodges that were far apart, too far apart, I thought. And this thought gave me an idea. Why not close that wide gap between those two lodges? Why not set up my little lodge between the two big ones, and shut this wide place up?

"While yet the horses were running around within the circle of the camp I dragged my poles to the spot, and quickly pitched my lodge there. I heard my mother calling me. I had to work very fast to shut up that wide place, believing that my little lodge would keep our horses from getting out, and the Lacota from getting in; but I did not finish pegging down my lodge-skin, not quite. Corn-woman found me. 'Ho! Ho!' she cried out, 'here is a brave little woman! She has shut the wide gap with her lodge. Ho! Ho!'

"But just the same she picked me up in her arms and carried me to my mother, as though I were a baby. Corn-woman told this story every year until she died.

"Now I shall have to tell you about the fighting, a little, because it was a woman's fight. A woman won it. The men never tell about it. They do not like to hear about it, but I am going to tell you what happened. I was there to see. And my eyes were good, too."

Pretty-shield, visibly moved by her thoughts, appeared to be almost angry. She got up, refolded her blanket deliberately, and then sat down upon it so decisively that I smiled.

"Yes," she said, shortly, "a woman won that fight, and the men never tell about it. There was shooting by the time my play-lodge was pitched. A Lacota bullet struck one of its poles, and whined. Arrows were coming among the lodges, and bullets, when Corn-woman carried me to my mother, who made me lie down behind a pack. I saw what went on there.

"Several horses were wounded and were screaming with their pain. One of them fell down near my mother's lodge that was not yet half pitched. Lying there behind that pack I did not cover my eyes. I was looking all the time, and listening to everything. I saw Strikes-two, a woman sixty years old, riding around the camp on a gray horse. She carried only her root-digger, and she was singing her medicine-song, as though Lacota bullets and arrows were not flying around her. I heard her say, 'Now all of you sing, "They are whipped. They are running away," and keep singing these words until I come back.'

"When the men and even the women began to sing as Strikes-two told them, she rode out straight at the Lacota, waving her root-digger and singing that song. I *saw* her, I *heard* her, and my heart swelled, because she was a woman.

"The Lacota, afraid of her medicine, turned and ran away. The fight was won, and by a woman," she said excitedly. Then, sorrowfully, "We lost three good men in the fighting. One of these, with a bullet in his lung, lived two days. A woman, a wise-one, named His-gun, who lately died here, tried to heal him; but something went wrong. I will tell you about it.

"His-gun had been called by the wounded man's family. Her medicine was a buffalo bull. She sent for four young girls, girls who were not yet women. I was one of them, so that I well remember all that happened.

"When I reached the lodge where the wounded man was lying on a robe, His-gun was already there, and painted with clay, the paint of buffalo bulls. She wore a bull's robe that had both head and tail, and there were feathers tied in her hair. Without speaking she placed two of us little girls on each side of the man, who was naked.

"In the lodge there were His-gun, the wounded man, two drummers, who are always men, and we four girls. Outside, the people had formed lines from the lodge-door to the river. They were all so still that I could hear the leaves stirring on the cottonwood trees, could almost hear my own heart, as I watched His-gun, who moved like a shadow.

"She lifted two bulls' tails, held them high for a moment, and then handed one of them to the wounded man, whose eyes were nearly dead. With the other tail she signaled the two drummers, and they began to beat their drums. His-gun, waving the tail, acted as a buffalo bull does when he is trying to lift something with his horns. At first she moved slowly, her body bending with her head, as though she were a buffalo bull that was trying to lift a heavy load. Then her movements grew faster and faster, until only her head was moving like a bull's head when he is lifting, lifting, lifting something with his horns. His-gun grunted as a bull does, 'Ummp, ummp, ummp, ummp!'

"Ahhh! The wounded man sat up. His eyes looked

more alive; and yet he appeared to be blind, to be feeling his way.

"His-gun stepped backward, one step, two steps, three steps, four steps. She was waving the bull's tail, her head moving even faster than before.

"The drummers, singing, 'The bull is here to heal the sick. He is going to make him get up and walk,' over and over and over, until I thought that every-body was singing; and then *I* sang, and the other girls sang, 'The bull is here to heal the sick. He is going to make him get up and walk.'

"I was watching as I never watched before. I saw the wounded man get up, stand on his feet, black blood dripping from a great hole near his heart, saw the big bullet fall out of it, and saw His-gun pick it up. The man walked. He followed His-gun out of the lodge, and into the river.

"These two entered the water, walked to the mid-dle of the stream, leaving the two drummers and us four little girls on the bank, singing, as we had been singing when we left the lodge.

"Whooooooo! Whooooooo!" Pretty-shield drummed her mouth with her open hand. "All the people did *that* when they saw the wounded man walk into the river behind His-gun," she said, her eyes brightened by remembrance.

"And His-gun kept grunting, as a buffalo bull grunts, 'Ummp, ummp,' until she stopped in the middle of the river. The water was above her waist a little. She stood downstream from the wounded man, who was taller than she was, bent down, and took water into her mouth. This she blew upon the man's breast, repeating four times; and all this time she was brushing the man's face with the bull's tail, held in her right hand.

"While all this was going on we four girls were singing, 'The bull is here to heal the sick. He is going to make him get up and walk.' And the drummers were singing these words; all the people were singing them.

"Suddenly His-gun held up her left hand. The singing stopped. The drumming stopped. I could hear the water rippling over the little stones near my feet. Ah, how still the world seemed while His-gun was leading the wounded man out of the water, and back into the lodge.

" 'I am sorry. My heart is heavy,' said His-gun, speaking to the wounded man, who sat down on a robe. 'I cannot heal you.' She looked tired. Her knees were trembling.

" 'I will smoke. Light a pipe for me,' said the wounded man, his words sounding far off.

"When he smoked, taking four deep draughts, I saw the tobacco smoke come out of the hole in his breast. Then he laid down, drew the end of his robe over his face, and went away forever. He was a good, brave man. We mourned for him."

She was silent now for several minutes. "There was something wrong that day," she mused, almost inaudibly. Then to me, "A man, a wise-one, had already tried to heal the wounded man before His-gun was called. I hoped His-gun might heal him, not only because he was a good man, but because His-gun was a woman. I wished this so much that I felt very tired when I left the lodge, nearly as tired as His-gun. I felt almost old."

She sighed heavily, straightening herself in her chair. "Where is the sun?" she asked after a moment. "I nearly forgot my grandchildren. They are hungry by now. I will come again in the morning."

SEVENTEEN

"How old did your friend, Plenty-coups, say he was?" Pretty-shield asked next day, apropos of nothing, so far as I could guess.

"Eighty-three," I said, thinking back, and adding the years since I had seen the aged chief.

"I think that he is eighty-nine, and Bell-rock ninety-three," she said, her eyes nearly closed, and her brow wrinkling. "I am going to tell you a story about Plenty-coups that he, himself, would not be likely to tell," she declared.

"I do not mean that he was to blame for what happened on the day I am going to tell you about. He could not have prevented it, because it was to be. And yet, as you will see, he would not wish to talk about it, or even think about it.

"Yes, I am sure that Plenty-coups is now eighty-nine," she mused, pressing her fist against the scar on her forehead. "I know that he had counted coup, and was a married man when I was yet a little girl. But I will tell my story.

"Once a woman, named Sitting-heifer, lost her

brother in a battle with the Lacota," she began. "She mourned for him until her friends felt afraid that she might die. Warriors gave her Lacota scalps, and black-paint, to help her forget her sorrow, but they did not heal her heart. At last, hoping to be happy again, she promised to give a sun-dance, a very serious thing for any woman to promise."

This "promise" or vow to "give a sun-dance," believed to be especially pleasing to the All High, is given to Him either in a spirit of thanksgiving for favors already received, or for desired blessings. The giver, or postulant, must be morally clean.

"Think of the meat and the work that must be given to make a sun-dance! More than one hundred buffalo tongues were needed to feed the warriors who had counted coup in battle, and who would tell their stories [recount their coups] and drum and sing in the sun-lodge. These buffalo tongues had to be dried, which required four sunny days; and four days are given by the warriors in preparing themselves to re-enact their coup-counting in the sun-lodge. Yes," she said, her face grave, "it is a serious thing to promise to give a sun-dance. There is always danger that some man or woman has lied.

"I believe this was the last time that our people gave a sun-dance. I watched the preparations as only the young can. The buffalo tongues were dry, the leaves on the trees fully grown [June], when the woman, Sitting-heifer, selected the spot for her sun-lodge. This was the very center of our village, whose lodges made a great circle on the green grass. I saw Calf-woman paint marks on the four poles, showing where they must be tied with a strip cut from a white buffalo robe. I watched, holding my breath, when the man, Big-otter, who tied the poles, was lifted upon them high into the air, knowing that if he had lied the strip of white buffalo robe would break and that he would fall and be killed.

"Up, up, went the poles, many men lifting Big-otter, who had tied the four poles together; up, up, while Big-otter stood on their tops, telling the people of his brave deeds, counting his many coups, and without lying, or he would have fallen. I held my breath watching the men lift Big-otter on these long poles high in the air.

"And then I smelled cooking meat. Four old women, whose faces were painted black and who had tied white breath-feathers in their hair, were boiling the dried buffalo tongues. The wind brought me the smell of the cooking meat; and Sitting-heifer must have smelled it more strongly than I did, because she had been fasting for four days and four nights.

"I saw Calf-woman paint Sitting-heifer with white clay. Even Sitting-heifer's buckskin dress was made snow white by Calf-woman, who worked very fast. Sitting-heifer, sick from her long mourning, weak from her fasting, looked bad when helped to her feet to walk to her sun-lodge. It was now that a man named No-death tried to persuade Sitting-heifer to turn back, to give up the four days of dancing. But she would not listen.

"I remember that for some unknown reason we all felt sad. Our hearts would not sing for this sun-dance as they had always sung for the others. And yet the dance went on, Sitting-heifer growing thinner and weaker until, on the fourth day, she could scarcely stand up to dance. Her eyes had no life left in them.

"The warriors kept coming into the sun-lodge where they acted their parts in battles, shooting arrows, and even guns that loaded from the front-ends. Their talking was loud and fierce, their actions wild as fighting wolves. The people all felt like a sinew bow-string that has been stretched too tightly. I breathed only in my throat.

"Sitting-heifer had to dance four times each day for four days. On the fourth day, when she was resting after her second dancing, Plenty-coups, who was already growing great, entered the sun-lodge with three other warriors. They came in on a charge: 'Whhhoooooo!' Plenty-coups gave the war-cry, aimed his gun, and *fired!*"

Pretty-shield, deeply affected, almost whispered the next two sentences. "The woman fell, her face looking up at the top of the sun-lodge. I heard her gasp; and then I ran away from there," she said, and was silent, her fingers rolling the corner of her blanket.

The scene, as I imagined it, held me fascinated, perhaps because I know Chief Plenty-coups so well.

"Her man's name was Long-ear," I heard Pretty-shield say in a voice that seemed intended for another to hear. "Sitting-heifer made a great mistake when she gave that sun-dance. She was not *fit* to give a sun-dance, and ought to have known this. She had once left three children, one of them a baby boy who died but three years ago," she went on, as though acknowledging the justice of fate.

She got up, and walked to the window. "I had better go to my place now," she said, abruptly, as a gust of wind set the windows rattling again. "My grand-children may be getting cold. I will come back," she promised from the door.

Within half an hour she was again sitting in her

chair beside our table, untying her black silk muffler. Without either complaint against the weather or the least comment on conditions at her "place," she asked, "What other things do you wish to ask me about, Sign-talker?"

"Tell me about Long-hair [a famous Crow chief]," I suggested.

She appeared almost shocked. "In the beginning you said that you wished me to tell only a woman's story. Do you now want me to tell you a *man's* story? Long-hair was a man, you know." She smiled, as though she enjoyed reminding me of my injunction. Then, without waiting for my answer, she began eagerly.

"My clan has furnished many great men and women. Long-hair was a Sore-lip, as I am. He was an orphan. His father and mother were killed by Cheyenne when he was yet a baby. He had a hard time getting along; and for some reason there was scarcely any hair on his head, so that there were jokes made about his appearance. He had no regular home, living a little here and there with his few relatives. He was not strong and he had few friends among children of his own age, so that he played few games. And yet, in some way, he became a cunning player of the hoop-and-arrow game. It was thought that he must have played by himself, since it was known that none of the young men ever asked to play with him.

"There was another young man who was also a smart player at the hoop-and-arrow game. This was Bird-comes-back. He was handsome, and a little too proud. Nevertheless he was a leader among those of his own age. People believed that some day he would become a chief.

"One day when the Crow village was on Thick-ash-trees [Reno creek] Bird-comes-back saw Long-hair playing alone at the hoop-and-arrow game, and laughed at his skill. 'I will play against you, if you have anything to bet,' he offered.

" 'I have a good horse,' said Long-hair, 'and I will bet him against one of yours that I think as good.'

"The news of the coming game spread over the village. In no time everybody came to watch Bird-comes-back play against Long-hair, the orphan boy.

"The hoop rolled. The players started, running beside it. Ho!"

Pretty-shield sprang up, seized an old broom that leaned against the wall by the stove, and holding the handle at "charge bayonets," sprang at me, as though I were the hoop. When I did not jump, as Goes-together had in the snake story, the old woman laughed so merrily that for a moment she forgot her tale.

"Yes," she finally went on, again sitting down, "and Long-hair won the game, and the horse of Bird-comes-back. Ho-ho! Bird-comes-back was both angry and ashamed. He spoke mean words, saying things to Long-hair that made the orphan boy's heart fall down. 'You are nobody,' he told Long-hair. 'You had better go away and try to dream. Look at your hair. Your head looks like a worn-out robe. Go first, and have a dream before you expect to play again with *me*.'

"Long-hair did not go back to the village with the other people. He sat there on the ground where he had won the hoop-and-arrow game until after the sun had come down to the world. Then he lifted up his robe, and went alone into the mountains, the words of Bird-comes-back making his heart a heavy load.

"At the foot of Wolf mountain he cut off the first finger of his left hand. By the time he reached the top of the mountain he had lost so much blood that his head was light as a breath-feather, and he fell down. His mind went away from him, and he slept. He saw a Man-person coming toward him; and then a Woman-person stood beside him. 'Ah, *you* are here, as usual,' said the Woman-person to the Man who was walking toward them. 'You *kill*. You ought not to have come here when you knew that I was coming to this young man.'

"The Woman-person was like a white cloud. The Man had light-colored hair and eyes. Four of his front teeth were like those of a bear, two above and two below. His forehead shone like a star; and yet he turned away, because the Woman-person did not want him there.

" 'Come, my son,' said the Woman-person, gently. And then Long-hair was in a beautiful lodge that at first was dark inside. It was night in there. Long-hair could see but little. An eagle sat at the head of the lodge, until the Woman-person spoke to him. Then the eagle went outside, and it was light in the lodge. It was daytime in there.

"Now, in the daylight, Long-hair saw the Man-person, the one with the light hair and eyes, and bear's teeth, sitting in the lodge with six other Persons, all of them women, and all looking like little white clouds that hang around mountain peaks. These seven Persons were seven generations.

" 'I heard what Bird-comes-back said to you, young man.'

"Long-hair looked quickly at the Man whose teeth

were like a bear's. Seven stars, The-many-together [the Little Dipper] shone in the middle of his forehead. It was he who had spoken.

" 'When you return to your people never speak words that will wound them,' said this Man-person. 'If Bird-comes-back asks you again to play the hoop-and-arrow game with him, refuse until he has asked the fourth time. Then, if you play with him, you will win everything that he possesses, even his woman. But before you play, before you have anything to do with him, or any of your people, take a sweat-bath, and wash your head. Then rub your hair with beaver oil and the musk of beavers. Do this every fourth day until sixteen days shall have passed, each time wrapping your head in the skin of a bighorn ram. Call in four of your clansmen to do this for you. On the twelfth day there will be a great change in your hair. I have spoken.'

"The Woman-person, the one who had come to him on the mountain, clapped her hands four times. Instantly a mountain-lion appeared. 'Take this young man, your brother, back to his people,' said the Woman-person; and then Long-hair found himself lying on the ground where he had fallen down after losing so much blood.

"A man, a Crow hunter, was standing over him. 'I

take you as my brother,' he said to Long-hair, helping him to stand. 'Come and live with me and my woman.'

"This man, this Crow hunter, helped Long-hair to reach the village where, living in his friend's lodge, he did all of the things that the Man-person, the one whose teeth looked like a bear's, had told him to do. When Bird-comes-back asked him to play the hoop-and-arrow game with him he said, 'No.' And when his friend, his new brother, urged him to play, saying, 'Take anything of mine, and bet it against him,' Long-hair said, 'No, not yet, brother.'

"When twelve days had passed, and the four clansmen of Long-hair's took the skin of the bighorn ram from his head, so that they might again rub on the beaver oil and the musk of beavers, they laid their hands upon their mouths [sign for astonishment]. His hair was long, longer than that of any other man in the Crow tribe.

" 'Speak no word of this until after the sixteenth day,' Long-hair told them; 'and burn more ground-cedar in this lodge. Let some of it be burning all day,' he requested, holding his head in the sweet-smelling smoke.

"On the sixteenth day, when the four clansmen were going to remove the skin of the bighorn ram from his head, Long-hair told them that his hair was to be one hundred hands long. When the skin of the bighorn ram was taken off, the four clansmen measured the hair that had grown on Long-hair's head in sixteen days. It was ninety-nine hands in length, reaching from the head of the lodge to the door, on both sides.

"Long-hair let it be known that he was ready to play the hoop-and-arrow game with Bird-comes-back, who had now asked for the game the fourth time. The village was again at Thick-ash-trees. The people, anxious to see a good game, even cut away the sage bushes, so that the hoop might roll swiftly. 'Bet nothing,' Long-hair advised the people; and yet he won every game that was played, until Bird-comes-back had nothing left to bet, not even his woman.

" 'Now,' said Long-hair, 'if Bird-comes-back is willing to bring to my lodge the medicine-pipe [apologize] I will return to him all the property that was his before we played the hoop-and-arrow game, even his woman, if she so wishes.

" 'No,' said the woman. 'No. I will never again live with Bird-comes-back.' And she never did. Her name was Good-calf, and she was a good woman.

"Long-hair died of smallpox. Forty lodges of people were with him, and all died. I believe that if his hair had grown to be one hundred hands long, as was intended, he would not have died as he did.

"I have made a mistake," said Pretty-shield, tapping the table-top with her fingers. "I said that *all* the people in those lodges died with Long-hair. I should have said all but four men, who had left the forty lodges to go to war against the Lacota.

"Plenty-coups, our chief, has the hair that grew in sixteen days on Long-hair's head," she confided. "I mean that he has nearly all of it. Each of the Crow clans has a little of this hair, because it is big medicine."

I have not seen this hair, and yet I know that Plenty-coups, the old chief, has it in his possession. Major General Hugh L. Scott, of the United States Army, retired, and Honorable Scott Leavitt, Representative from Montana in Congress, saw the hair in the fall of 1930 and examined it. Besides this, they saw it measured. It was seventy-six hands in length, or, allowing four inches to a hand, a little more than twenty-five feet. If, as Pretty-shield declares, some of it had been cut off, and given to the various Crow clans, it may have been originally ninety-nine hands long.[1]

[1] I append at the end of the book a letter from Congressman Scott Leavitt written in reply to my request for verification of the measurement of this hair.

"Yes, the Sore-lips have furnished many great men and women," Pretty-shield continued. "There was No-mane, whose medicine was the evening-star [the Crows call this the Day-star, because, while it belongs to the night, it likes the day best], Knocks-it-down, whose medicine was the morning-star [called by the Crows, Sees-the-ground], Long-hair, whose medicine was the sun, White-head, whose medicine was The-seven-stars [Big Dipper], Walks-with-the-moon, whose medicine was the moon, and Good-clothes, a woman, whose medicine was Red-woman; and she acted like Red-woman, too. She had no children, lived alone, and was wise. And yet, when I was a little girl she often frightened me. I was afraid of her. She lived to be so old that her skin cracked. She always wore four blue beads on her wrists. I have one of the beads to this day."

EIGHTEEN

"Goes-ahead was with General Custer on the day he was killed on the Little Bighorn, was he not?"

"Ahh," she smiled, with great pride in her eyes, "and for that the Great Chief in Washington sends me, every moon, a paper that I trade away for thirty dollars. And I need it for my grandchildren. I wish it were more," she added, a quick change in her expressive face.

"Tell me about this," I urged. "Tell me all that

222

you remember about the fight on the Little Bighorn."

She got up and went to the door, stood there looking out at the hill that is thickly covered with gleam-
ing white monuments marking the supposed spots
where, on the twenty-fifth of June, 1876, General
Custer, and Troops C, E, I, F, and L, of the famous
Seventh United States Cavalry, died to the last man.

"Were they ever buried?" I asked, standing behind
her.

"I do not know, Sign-talker," she answered, with
uncertainty in her voice. "I do know that this coun-

try smelled of dead men for a whole summer after the fight, and that we moved away from here, because we could not stand it. Ahh, war is bad," she sighed, turning back into our room. "There was always somebody missing, because of war.

"I was a young woman when Son-of-the-morningstar [General Custer] fought our old enemies, the Lacota and Cheyenne, on the Little Bighorn," she went on, speaking slowly, as though collecting her thoughts. "Many of our young men went with The-other-one [General Terry]. More than one hundred, maybe fifty more, went with Three-stars [General Crook], who got whipped on the Rosebud by Crazyhorse and his warriors. Besides these many Crows went with Son-of-the-morning-star. These are the ones that you have asked me to tell you about. I will begin at the beginning.

"We were camped above the mouth of Rotten-sundance-tepee [Clark Fork] when some blue soldiers came to ask our chief for some wolves [scouts]. These blue soldiers came to us in a fire-boat on the Elk river [Yellowstone]. It was in the moon when leaves were showing [May], and our chief gave a feast to our visitors who talked with our warriors in council.

"I, being a woman, did not hear what was said there. But after the talking twenty-five of our young men promised to meet the blue soldiers at the mouth of Tongue river. Half-yellow-face, my uncle, carried their pipe [was their leader]. The second night, when these Crows, who were going to be wolves for the blue soldiers, camped near the spot now occupied by the city of Forsyth, the Lacota stole every horse that they had, every one. The Crows were *afoot*," she chuckled, "and they had not yet seen the white man's war; and my man, Goes-ahead, was with them."

These thoughts contributed much to her merriment. "Ahh, the Lacota were cunning horse-thieves," she admitted. "Tst, tst, tst! Yes, the Lacota could steal horses almost as cunningly as the Crows. We always had many Lacota horses, sometimes hundreds of them," she laughed. "But I am forgetting my story.

"Somebody had now to go back to the Crow village for horses before these Crow wolves could go on to the white man's war," she continued. "And when the two who came for horses left our village, twelve more young warriors went with them to join the waiting-ones who were afoot. These Crow wolves had no interpreter with them, so that when the party finally reached the blue soldiers at the mouth of the Tongue river, a half-breed Lacota talked for them there. [Probably Frank Gruard, said to be a Sandwich

Islander, whom the Indian believed to be a half-breed Sioux.]

"Our village, a large one with many, many lodges and large herds of horses, moved to The-long-drop. It was here that a Shoshone warrior came to us, asking for some more Crows. He told our men that a big blue soldier chief, named Three-stars [General Crook] had many, many men on Goose creek, where the city of Sheridan, Wyoming, stands today. This Shoshone said that his own people were going to help this big soldier chief to whip the Lacota and Cheyenne, and that this chief, Three-stars, wanted some Crows to join him, to be with him when he wiped out our old enemies. But he did not wipe them out. Instead, he got a good whipping himself. And, of course, the Crows and the Shoshones, who were with him, got a good whipping, too. And yet I believe that they did better work, that they fought harder, than the blue soldiers, who picked a bad place for their fight with Crazy-horse on the Rosebud.

"But I know only what my man, Goes-ahead, told me after the white man's war was finished. Anyhow more than a hundred, perhaps nearly one hundred and fifty, of our young men went away with this Shoshone wolf that Three-stars had sent to our village. [Plenty-coups says one hundred and thirty.] Plenty-coups, who was then a young chief, and very brave, carried the pipe for these Crow wolves. Besides Plenty-coups, there were Flathead-woman, Medicine-crow, and Alligator-stands-up, all strong leaders and brave men, who went with the others to help Three-stars, the blue soldier chief, who was waiting for them on Goose creek.

"I cannot tell you about the fighting. I remember that they brought Bull-snake back to us badly wounded, and that many blue soldiers who had been with Three-stars were killed. I remember, too, that we moved our village to Yellow-willows [near Powell, of today] to be out of the way. There were not many young warriors left with us. There were many old men and some young boys, so that we kept rather quiet in the village at Yellow-willows until our men returned. It was here at this camp on Yellow-willows that the Crow warriors who had been with Three-stars reached us, after the fighting. The big village that had been so quiet now became lively again. And how quickly the women looked to see if their men had come back to them."

Here Pretty-shield paused, a quizzical look in her eyes. Leaning toward me she asked in a half whisper, "Did the men ever tell you anything about a woman who fought with Three-stars on the Rosebud?"

"No," I replied, wondering.

"Ahh, they do not like to tell of it," she chuckled. "But I will tell you about it. We Crows all know about it. I shall not be stealing anything from the men by telling the truth.

"Yes, a Crow woman fought with Three-stars on the Rosebud, *two* of them did, for that matter; but one of them was neither a man nor a woman. She looked like a man, and yet she wore woman's clothing; and she had the heart of a woman. Besides, she did a woman's work. Her name was Finds-them-and-kills-them. She was not a man, and yet not a woman," Pretty-shield repeated. "She was not as strong as a man, and yet she was wiser than a woman," she said, musingly, her voice scarcely audible.

"The other woman," she went on, "was a *wild* one who had no man of her own. She was both bad and brave, this one. Her name was The-other-magpie; and she was pretty.

"I have said that I know nothing about the fighting on the Rosebud, except what my man, Goes-ahead, told me. When I saw the big party of Crow wolves, who had been with Three-stars, coming back from the war, they were all singing. This told us that they had been lucky. I saw the two women, Finds-them-and-kills-them, and The-other-magpie, riding and singing with them. Finds-them-and-kills-them had a gun, and The-other-magpie a long coup-stick, with one breath-feather on its small end.

"During the fight on the Rosebud both these women did brave deeds. When Bull-snake fell from his horse, badly wounded, Finds-them-and-kills-them dashed up to him, got down from her horse, and stood over him, shooting at the Lacota as rapidly as she could load her gun and fire. The-other-magpie rode round and round them, singing her war-song and waving her coup-stick, the only weapon she had. When the Lacota, seeing Bull-snake on the ground, charged to take his scalp, The-other-magpie rode straight at them, waving her coup-stick. Her medicine was so strong that the Lacota turned and rode away; and Bull-snake was saved. All the men saw these things, and yet they have never told you about them.

"Both these women expected death that day. Finds-them-and-kills-them, afraid to have the Lacota find her dead with woman-clothing on her, changed them to a man's before the fighting commenced, so that if killed the Lacota would not laugh at her, lying there with a woman's clothes on her. She did not want the Lacota to believe that she was a Crow man hiding in a woman's dress, you see.

"Yes, Sign-talker, there was a woman and a *half*-woman who fought on the Rosebud with Three-stars. The woman, I remember, wore a stuffed woodpecker on her head, and her forehead was painted yellow. Her coup-stick was big medicine that day, and she rode a black horse. She went to the war because her brother had lately been killed by the Lacota. She wanted to get even, and she did. Riding straight at the Lacota, with only her coup-stick, she spat at them: 'See,' she called out, 'my spit is my arrows.' She rode against a Lacota's horse, even struck the Lacota with her coup-stick, counting a coup on him, just as Finds-them-and-kills-them fired with her gun, and killed him. When the Lacota fell The-other-magpie took his scalp. She was waving it when I saw her coming into the village with the others. Yes, and I saw her cut this scalp into many pieces, so that the men might have more scalps to dance with."

Pretty-shield had been speaking rapidly, her dark eyes snapping. Now she leaned back in her chair. "Ahh," she said a little bitterly, "the men did not tell you this; but *I* have. And it's the truth. Every old Crow, man or woman, knows that it is the truth."

And then as though she feared that she might have been unfair, "I am sure that your friend, Plenty-coups, has told you only the truth. But if he left *this* out he did not tell you all of the truth," she added quite severely. "Two women, one of them not quite a woman, fought with Three-stars, and I hope that you will put it in a book, Sign-talker, because it is the truth.

"The return of the Crow wolves and these two women to our village was one of the finest sights that I have ever seen," she continued, excitement gone from her eyes. "I felt proud of the two women, even of the wild one, because she was brave. And I saw that they were the ones who were taking care of Bull-snake, the wounded man, when they rode in.

"Ahh, there was great rejoicing. And of course we had a big scalp-dance. I think that the party had taken ten scalps besides the one that The-other-magpie cut into so many pieces, so there were enough for many dancers. We women, who had felt a little afraid with so many warriors gone, began now to be gay, where before we had been quiet. There was feasting on fat meat, and the big dance that lasted all night. The drums! Ahh, I liked to hear the drums, because when they were beating loudly our hearts were light as breath-feathers. And yet on this night my own man, Goes-ahead, was not with us. He was with Son-of-the-morning-star [General Custer] and the other soldier chiefs at the mouth of Tongue river.

I wished him back. In those days women were always wishing that their men were back from war, or from horse-stealing raids against the Lacota, or the Pecunnie, or the Arapahoe, or the Cheyenne. And yet they were such happy days!

"Now, after all this traveling around, I am coming to what you wished to know, the fight on the Little Bighorn. When Son-of-the-morning-star left the camp of the blue soldiers at the mouth of Tongue river he went up the Rosebud. My man, Goes-ahead, White-swan, Half-yellow-face, Hairy-moccasin, White-man-runs-him, and Curly were his wolves. The country was filled with Lacota and Cheyenne. They were like ants on a freshly killed buffalo robe that is pegged to the ground. Of course the Crow wolves knew this by the *sign* that the enemy left, tracks, old fires, and dead buffalo whose meat had been but half taken, many such things that told the truth. Such things tell a good deal, show that men are traveling, and that they are in a great hurry to reach some place.

"My man, Goes-ahead, White-man-runs-him, and Hairy-moccasin, were ahead of Son-of-the-morning-star and his blue horse-soldiers. Half-yellow-face, who was my uncle, and carried the pipe [commanded], and Curly were with Son-of-the-morning-star. Curly

said that he was sick, and I guess he was. Maybe what
he knew was ahead of him made him sick. It was
enough to make anybody feel a little like lying down
for a while.

"Do you know where Busby is?" she asked,
suddenly.

"Yes," I said.

"Well, Busby wasn't there in those days," she
laughed. "But at that point the three Crows, wolves,
who were ahead of Son-of-the-morning-star saw
sign that told them many, many Lacota lodges had
been there, and that they had not been long gone.
Some of their fires were yet smoking a little; and the
three Crow wolves found a few Lacota horses there,
too. These they caught. This camp was the very one
that had whipped Three-stars, but nobody then knew
that he had been whipped by Crazy-horse and his
warriors on the Rosebud.

"My man, Goes-ahead, Hairy-moccasin, and White-
man-runs-him, knew that there were more Lacota and
Cheyenne somewhere ahead than there were bullets in
the belts of the blue soldiers who were with Son-of-
the-morning-star. They believed that they ought to
tell him this, so they went back, and told him. But
he only said, 'Go on again,' and then drank from a
straw-covered bottle that was on his saddle.

"My man, Goes-ahead, and the other two Crow wolves, went on again, as they had been told. But when they came, once more, to the place where the big Lacota village had been, they waited there for Son-of-the-morning-star to come to them with his horse-soldiers. They knew that there were too many Lacota and Cheyenne ahead, and were afraid to go on alone.

"When he got there, and had looked around a little, Son-of-the-morning-star asked my man, Goes-ahead, if there was a better place to camp near there. Goes-ahead said that there was, that at a creek white men call Thompson there was a better place. The water that is in this creek comes from the high mountain springs, and is cool and good.

"The blue horse-soldiers went to this creek and made their camp. Before the next morning came the Crow wolves were again out, looking for the Lacota and Cheyenne. The sun was not yet near the middle of the sky when they saw the biggest village they had ever looked upon in their lives. It was on the Little Bighorn river. The flat was white with lodges, and the hills black with Lacota and Cheyenne horses, as far as they could see.

"My man, Goes-ahead, told me that he felt afraid when he saw so many lodges. He, with the two others,

Hairy-moccasin, and White-man-runs-him, turned here, going up the creek that white men call Reno. They met Son-of-the-morning-star coming down this creek, and told him what they had seen. They said that there were more Lacota, more enemies, than there were bullets in the soldiers' belts, that there were too many to fight.

"But Son-of-the-morning-star was going to his death, and did not know it. He was like a feather blown by the wind, and *had* to go."

She pressed her fist against her forehead, and bent her head. "Tst, tst, tst! He would not listen," she murmured. "And he was brave; yes, he was a brave man.

"Two-bodies, a half-breed interpreter, listened," she went on [probably Mitch Boyer]. He spoke to Son-of-the-morning-star, saying, 'You can yet get safely away.'

"But the soldier chief wanted to fight. He *had* to fight, because he had to *die*. And this made others die with him," she added, speaking slowly and with deep feeling.

"My man, Goes-ahead, told me that Son-of-the-morning-star drank too often from the straw-covered bottle, and that as soon as Two-bodies told him that he might yet get away he made a big mistake by dividing his blue horse-soldiers into three parties, sending two of them away from him."

Pretty-shield was deeply affected here. She stood up, leaning over the table. "It was now that my man, Goes-ahead, stripped himself for battle, tying some breath-feathers in his hair," she said, speaking rapidly. "And it was now that the little chief, Reno, went away as he had been ordered, with all of the Arickara wolves. White-swan and Half-yellow-face went with them, by mistake. And it was now that Curly, who said he was sick, ran away. Ahh, I know these things are true, because my man, Goes-ahead, was there and saw them happen.

"Reno, the little soldier chief, crossed the river and began shooting. Then he ran away, because he saw how the fight would end. Anybody would have known its end, *anybody*.

"My man, Goes-ahead, was with Son-of-the-morning-star when he rode down to the water of the Little Bighorn. He heard a Lacota call out to Two-bodies, who rode beside Son-of-the-morning-star, and say, 'Go back, or you will die.'

"But Son-of-the-morning-star did not go back. He went *ahead*, rode *into the water of the Little Bighorn*, with Two-bodies on one side of him, and his flag on the other—and he *died* there, *died in the water of the*

236

Little Bighorn, with Two-bodies, and the blue soldier carrying his flag.

"When he fell in the water, the other blue soldiers ran back up the hill. It was now that my man, Goes-ahead, ran fast. He told me that the fighters were so many, and so crazy, that in the thick dust and powder-smoke, anybody might easily have run away. So he, White-man-runs-him, and Hairy-moccasin, ran when they saw Son-of-the-morning-star fall into the water, with Two-bodies and the blue horse-soldier that carried his flag. My man, Goes-ahead, showed me where Son-of-the-morning-star fell into the water. [Mitch Boyer, called Two-bodies by the Crows, was a half-breed interpreter. He was killed with General Custer.]

"They ran up the little creek that comes into the Little Bighorn just above the spot where Son-of-the-morning-star fell down from his horse. I will take you there, and show you. They kept running fast until they came to the packers, who had all the blue soldiers' bullets and grub. My man, Goes-ahead, said that when he got there with Hairy-moccasin and White-man-runs-him the packers had formed a circle with their pack-train, and that the mules were falling dead, that bullets were coming like rain, and that he, with the two other Crow wolves, stopped there to help the

237

packers fight. They dug pits there, and beside these holes, the dead mules stopped many, many bullets. My man, Goes-ahead, said that, with the packers, they killed more Lacota and Cheyenne than the blue soldiers did."

Gradually, as she talked, her voice had grown louder, her position more tense. "Ahh," she sighed, suddenly relaxing, "my man, Goes-ahead, told me that he was afraid; and yet he did not run away until he saw Son-of-the-morning-star fall down from his horse into the water of the Little Bighorn. He told me that Son-of-the-morning-star was ahead of his men, and that when he fell the blue horse-soldiers ran back up the hill. He took me to the place, and showed me exactly where Son-of-the-morning-star fell into the water, with Two-bodies and the flag, where he himself started to run away, and where he stopped to fight with the packers. Yes," she said, her voice trailing off to a murmur, "my man, Goes-ahead, was afraid that day; but he did not lie to *me*. The monument that white men have set up to mark the spot where Son-of-the-morning-star fell down, is a lie. He fell in the water," she whispered, as though to the shade of her man, Goes-ahead.

Her attitude affected me deeply. Goes-together, our interpreter, who had been sewing buckskin with an awl and sinew, laid her work aside, as though she too had been stirred by Pretty-shield's expressed feeling. When the old woman again spoke her words startled me.

"The sun was more than half way between the middle of the sky and the world when the yelling and shooting stopped," she said, evenly. "It was now that White-man-runs-him spoke in Crow to my man, Goes-ahead, and Hairy-moccasin. 'We had better get away from here before the enemy charges this place,' he said.

"The three Crow wolves got up to go. They had good soldiers' guns now, and thought that they could make out to reach their people.

" 'Where are you going?' the chief packer asked.

" 'We are going to get a drink of water,' signed White-man-runs-him, cunningly.

"The packer chief gave each of the three Crow wolves a canvas-covered, flat bottle to fill and bring back. But every man who had tried to fill one of those bottles had been killed, every one. The three Crows did not go after the water, did not even keep the flat bottles. They cut across to Reno creek, following it upstream until they reached pine trees. Here they saw four Lacota wolves who had been sitting on the high hills to watch for more blue soldiers. They had not been in the fighting. One of these Lacota wolves was quite a way behind the others. He was riding a gray horse, and leading a sorrel mule that must have got away from the blue soldiers. My man, Goes-ahead, killed this Lacota, and scalped him. The sorrel mule got away from Goes-ahead, but not the gray horse. The rope that the dead Lacota had dropped when my man's bullet struck him, got tangled in the gray's legs, so that Goes-ahead caught him. He gave this horse to White-man-runs-him. They took turns riding him, because they had no other horse. They had lost them in the fight. I well remember that old gray Lacota horse. His back was sore, and he was so old that he was no good.

"This all happened in the moon when the leaves are fully grown [June]. When my man, Goes-ahead, reached the Bighorn river with the two others, he found it high, bad to cross. The water had spread out very wide. Rain was falling, and it was dark besides. The point where they reached the Bighorn was where the city of Hardin stands now. They could not see the other side of the wide river when they began to swim, so that when they reached land they thought that they were across the stream. But it was only an island they reached; and here they rested before going the rest of the way.

"They had no clothes, because they had stripped themselves to fight, and did not go back to look for any clothes. But now they felt pretty cold, and they were hungry, having had nothing to eat since the morning before the fighting on the Little Bighorn. While they were resting the day came, gray and rainy. Goes-ahead saw two wolves on the hills across the Bighorn. He believed they were Crows, but the others thought them Lacota. Anyhow Goes-ahead called loudly, and then made signs. The two wolves across the Bighorn were Crows, as Goes-ahead had believed. They came down to the water's edge on their side, and said, in signs, that all the blue horse-soldiers were dead.

"One of these Crow wolves, who had been with The-limping-one [General Gibbon] was named No-milk. The other's name was Plenty-butterflies. No-milk crossed the river and gave my man and the others some bacon and soldiers' bread, and part of his clothing. He said that more blue soldiers, walking-soldiers, were coming, and that they had six wagons with them that made their traveling very slow. He said that the soldiers had told him that White-swan, and my uncle, Half-yellow-face, the two Crow wolves who had, by mistake, gone with the little soldier-chief [Reno] when Son-of-the-morning-star divided his men, were dead. While he was talking some other

Crows who had been with The-limping-one [Gibbon] and The-other-one [Terry] crossed the river, and did not go back to the walking-soldiers.

"Our village was on Arrow creek [Pryor] when these Crows came to us. When our wolves saw them they signaled that the Lacota were coming. A war-party rode out to meet them, and even attacked them, by mistake. My man, Goes-ahead, had to kill two of their horses before the Crow war-party saw its mistake and stopped its foolishness. By this you can see how nervous my people were during these days of trouble. Everybody looked exactly like a Lacota to us.

"This time the home-coming of our warriors was not a happy one. I saw my man, Goes-ahead, and felt glad; but when the men who had been to war told us that Half-yellow-face and White-swan were dead, my heart fell down to the ground. They were both good, brave men, and besides, Half-yellow-face was my uncle, my father's brother. The mourning was terrible to hear. The relatives of the two missing men gave away all their horses, and clothing, cutting themselves on their arms and legs and heads until they were bloody all over. But when my father began to mourn for his brother, Half-yellow-face, my man, Goes-ahead, stopped him. 'Wait four days,' he said, 'and

242

then if your brother does not return I will mourn with you.'

"All that night the people mourned, crying for their dead, and for Son-of-the-morning-star, and his blue soldiers, who had so foolishly died."

She ended, abruptly, staring at the wall over my head. "Sign-talker," she said, severely, "too much drinking may have made that great soldier-chief foolish on that day when he died. I have seen whisky do such things. Our own chiefs have signed too many papers with their thumbs when whisky was doing their thinking for them. Our old men were not whisky drinkers. The first time that I ever saw a Crow warrior drink whisky was when a fire-boat blew up on the Big river. There were many barrels of whisky along the river there, after that fire-boat sank in the water; and some of our men drank a little and grew foolish, so foolish that we all laughed at them. But lately our men drink, and do not care who laughs."

"Tell me about Half-yellow-face and White-swan and Curly," I suggested, to get her back to her story.

"Ahh, Curly did not come back for a long time," she said. "He found the blue soldiers who were with The-other-one and The-limping-one, and went with them to the place where the big fighting had been. It was not until after some white men took him to

Washington that Curly talked, and then his tongue was not very straight.

"When Half-yellow-face and White-swan got back we heard their story, and it was like hearing the dead speak, because we thought they had been killed. They said that they had not understood, and had gone with the little chief [Reno] by mistake. They were with him until his men came to the big Lacota village, until the little chief's men got off their horses to shoot, and until one of the littler chiefs tried to get back onto his horse, and got dragged. He let his foot go clear through the stirrup, and his frightened horse ran away, dragging him. When Half-yellow-face and White-swan saw this they knew it was bad medicine. They saw how things were going to end, as anybody could; and then they ran to a hole in the hill. My man, Goes-ahead, showed me this hole, and so did my uncle, Half-yellow-face; and I will show it to you.

"The Lacota set the country afire to drive them out of the hole. It was here that White-swan got shot in the hand. His hand was never any good after that day. He was also shot in the foot and in the shoulder. But the bullet only burned his shoulder, making a bloody mark there that was not bad. They stayed in that hole, even when the smoke of the Lacota fire nearly smothered them, for two days and two nights;

and some of the Arickara wolves were in there with them.

"Finally the Lacota and Cheyenne left the Little Bighorn, and then the walking-soldiers came. Half-yellow-face said that they were very glad to see the walking-soldiers, because White-swan's wounds were swelling, and looked very bad, and because they all wanted to get something to eat."

She hesitated a little now, and then as though to wipe away any possibly detracting statement that she had made about General Custer, she said: "Even if Son-of-the-morning-star had not divided his men he would have been whipped and killed, because he was being blown by the winds. If The-other-one, Three-stars, The-limping-one, and Son-of-the-morning-star had kept together they would have whipped the Lacota and Cheyenne; but no one of them could have done this. There were too many Lacota, too many Cheyenne.

"Two years after this bad day Half-yellow-face took my man, Goes-ahead, and me, over the ground where all these things happened. I can take you over it, and tell you exactly what he told us. Yes," she added, "and for more than a year my people found dead blue soldiers and dead Lacota far from the Little Bighorn. I remember that in the summer following the big fight my people found four blue soldiers together, one of them a chief, beyond Big-shoulder, on Bear-in-the-middle creek. This is six miles from the fighting-place on the Little Bighorn. Our men said that, by the clothes he wore, they knew that one of these dead horse-soldiers was a chief."

Here, suddenly reminded of her duty, Pretty-shield stood up, her blanket falling to the floor. "Ahh!" she exclaimed, glancing at the window, "the sun is low down. I have talked about war until I forgot my grandchildren. I will come again. Ho!"

Having business of my own at the Trader's store, I followed Pretty-shield there; and was glad that I did, because her short visit had inspired an Indian of about sixty years to talk to the trader about her man, Goes-ahead.

"Goes-ahead took me there, and showed me where General Custer fell in the water," he was saying, in pidgin English, when I entered. "And he showed me where he and White-man-runs-him and Hairy-moccasin ran up a little creek that is there, where they found the packers with their pack-train, and stopped to fight," he went on. "Yes," he said, "and when I was a young man I knew Big-nose, a Lacota who told me that he, himself, killed General Custer, and that the General fell in the water, with his half-breed interpreter, a man that the Crows called Two-bodies. His white name was Mitch Boyer, I guess."

There was more, most of it of little importance to me, except the telling of finding the bodies of four cavalrymen six miles from the battlefield on the Little Bighorn, the man declaring that his father had been one of the Crows who found them. "One of these dead soldiers was an officer," he said, thus strengthening Pretty-shield's story. I had not doubted that she had related exactly, and in detail, her man's experiences on the day of the battle of the Little Bighorn, and yet I was glad to get this uninvited corroboration.

NINETEEN

I WONDERED if I could get Pretty-shield to talk of the days when her people were readjusting themselves to present conditions. Plenty-coups, the aged Chief, had refused to speak of the days that immediately followed the passing of the buffalo, saying: "When the buffalo went away the hearts of my people fell to the ground, and they could not lift them up again. After this nothing happened. There was little singing anywhere. Besides, you know that part of my life as well as I do. You saw what happened to us when the buffalo went away."

Now I asked Pretty-shield, "How old were you when the buffalo disappeared?"

She hesitated. "Tst, tst, tst! I haven't seen a buffalo in more than forty years," she said slowly, as though she believed herself to be dreaming.

"The happiest days of my life were spent following the buffalo herds over our beautiful country. My mother and father and Goes-ahead, my man, were all kind, and we were so happy. Then, when my children came I believed I had everything that was good on this world. There were always so many, many buf-falo, plenty of good fat meat for everybody.

"Since my man, Goes-ahead, went away twelve snows ago my heart has been falling down. I am old now, and alone, with so many grandchildren to watch," she interposed, and fell silent.

"I do not hate *anybody*, not even the white man," she said, as though she had been accused by her con-science. "I have never let myself hate the white man, because I knew that this would only make things worse for me. But he changed everything for us, did many bad deeds before we got used to him.

"Sign-talker," she said, leaning toward me, "white cowboys met a deaf and dumb Crow boy on the plains, and because he could not answer their ques-tions, could not even hear what they said, they roped him and dragged him to death."

"Tell me what happened when the buffalo went away," I urged.

"Sickness came, strange sickness that nobody knew about, when there was no meat," she said, covering her face with both hands as though to shut out the sight of suffering. "My daughter stepped into a horse's track that was deep in the dried clay, and hurt her ankle. I could not heal her; nobody could. The white doctor told me that the same sickness that makes people cough themselves to death was in my daughter's ankle. I did not believe it, and yet she died, leaving six little children. Then my other daughter died, and left hers. These things would not have happened if we Crows had been living as we were intended to live. But how could we live in the old way when everything was gone?

"Ahh, my heart fell down when I began to see dead buffalo scattered all over our beautiful country, killed and skinned, and left to rot by white men, many, many hundreds of buffalo. The first I saw of this was in the Judith basin. The whole country there smelled of rotting meat. Even the flowers could not put down the bad smell. Our hearts were like stones. And yet nobody believed, even then, that the white man could kill *all* the buffalo. Since the beginning of things there had always been so many! Even the Lacota, bad as their hearts were for us, would not do such a thing as this; nor the Cheyenne, nor the Arapahoe, nor the Pecunnie; and yet the white man did this, even when he did not want the meat.

"We believed for a long time that the buffalo would again come to us; but they did not. We grew hungry and sick and afraid, all in one. Not believing their own eyes our hunters rode very far looking for buffalo, so far away that even if they had found a herd we could not have reached it in half a moon. 'Nothing; we found nothing,' they told us; and then, hungry, they stared at the empty plains, as though dreaming. After this their hearts were no good any more. If the Great White Chief in Washington had not given us food we should have been wiped out without even a chance to fight for ourselves.

"And then white men began to fence the plains so that we could not travel; and anyhow there was now little good in traveling, nothing to travel for. We began to stay in one place, and to grow lazy and sicker all the time. Our men had fought hard against our enemies, holding them back from our beautiful country by their bravery; but now, with everything else going wrong, we began to be whipped by weak foolishness. Our men, our leaders, began to drink the white man's whisky, letting it do their thinking. Because we were used to listening to our chiefs in the buffalo days, the days of war and excitement, we listened to them now; and we got whipped. Our wise-ones became fools, and drank the white man's whisky. But what else was there for us to do? We knew no other way than to listen to our chiefs and head men. Our old men used to be different; even our children were different when the buffalo were here.

"Tst, tst, tst! We were given a reservation, a fine one, long ago. We had many, many horses, and even cattle that the Government had given us. We might have managed to get along if the White Chief in Washington had not leased our lands to white stockmen. These men, some of them, shot down our horses on our own lands, because they wanted all the grass for themselves.

"Yes," she went on, her eyes snapping, "these white men shot down our horses so that their cows and sheep might have the grass. They even paid three dollars for each pair of horse's ears, to get our horses killed. It was as though our horses, on our own lands, were wolves that killed the white men's sheep."

She quickly curbed the anger that these thoughts had aroused. "I have not long to stay here," she said, solemnly. "I shall soon be going away from this world; but my grandchildren will have to stay here for a long time yet. I wonder how they will make out. I wonder if the lease-money that is paid to the Government in Washington by the white stockmen will be given to my grandchildren when it is paid in, or if they will have to wear out their moccasins going to the Agency office to ask for it, as I do.

"But then," she added quickly, the light of fun leaping to her eyes, "I suppose they will be wearing the white man's shoes, because shoes last longer than moccasins."

I felt that my work was finished now. Outside, our backs turned to the cutting March wind that was whipping the cottonwood, I said good-bye to Goes-together; and then Pretty-shield and I walked across the Agency square to the store.

"Fire is good today," she signed, spreading her hands to the warmth of the Trader's big stove. Then, a little regretfully I thought, she asked. "When are you traveling?"

"Tonight," I signed, adding, "You and I are friends, Pretty-shield."

"Bard-ners," she said earnestly, in pidgin English.

May her moccasins make tracks in many snows that are yet to come.

APPENDIX

CONGRESS OF THE UNITED STATES
HOUSE OF REPRESENTATIVES
WASHINGTON, D. C.

Great Falls, Montana,
June 10, 1931.

Hon. Frank B. Linderman,
Somers, Montana.

My dear Frank:

Further reference is made to my letter of May 29th. I have now received from my Washington office a copy of the letter I wrote General Scott last January, which was based on the notes I made at the time of our visit to Plenty Coups. I have wished to confirm my memory as to the exact length of the lock of hair from the head of Long Hair.

On the 22nd of September, 1930, Major General Hugh L. Scott and myself were guests of Plenty

Coups at his home near Pryor. We had taken part the day before in the dedication of a marker at the old fort near Hardin and had been informed then that Plenty Coups desired us to come to his home.

As you know, the old chief has an upper chamber in his home in which he keeps the things sacred to himself, such as his medicine bundle. He received us there. There were two Crow women, a blind Indian, and Max Big Man, a Crow, besides General Scott and myself who witnessed and took part in the ceremony of purification performed by Plenty Coups before the opening of the medicine bundle and the unwrapping of the lock of hair. The old chief uttered a ceremonial prayer, washed his hands in the smoke of pine needles and rubbed them with beaver musk. With the smoke he also purified his breast and arms. The beaver musk was passed around the circle for use on all of our hands before we were privileged to touch the lock of hair.

Finally Plenty Coups unrolled the bundle and removed the wrappings from the lock of hair. It was rolled in an open circle, wrapped in many colors of cloth and finally with buckskin, all of which he very reverently removed and then began to unwind the lock of hair. As the hair was unrolled it was passed from hand to hand around the circle until its entire length was displayed, and Max Big Man measured it with his hands, placing one after the other. The lock of hair measured seventy-six hands and the width of one of Big Man's fingers. This would prove it to be over twenty-five feet long. There was no evidence of any joining together of various locks. The reverence with which it was handled and regarded by Plenty Coups, whose deep sincerity is so well known to yourself, was further and conclusive proof to me that the lock is genuine. I have never felt more greatly honored than when Plenty Coups told us through Max Big Man that General Scott and myself were the first white men ever to be shown and allowed to touch this lock of hair.

I regret a little delay in making final reply, entirely due to my desire to check up on my memory as to the exact length of the lock of hair.

With sincerest personal regards and well wishes,

Very truly yours,

SCOTT LEAVITT.